THE
Quilter's
HANDBOOK

THE Quilter's HANDBOOK

Edited by Rosemary Wilkinson

Photographs by Shona Wood

Martingale
& COMPANY
Bothell, Washington

Martingale
& COMPANY

*That Patchwork Place is an imprint of
Martingale & Company.*

Martingale & Company, PO Box 118
Bothell, WA 98041-0118 USA
www.patchwork.com

Created and produced by
Rosemary Wilkinson Publishing

Library of Congress Cataloging-in
Publication Data available.

ISBN 1-56477-293-4

Art editor: Ruth Prentice
Illustrators: Carol Hill, Kate Simunek
Computer diagrams: Stephen Dew
Templates: Len Whiteman

Reproduction by PICA Colour
Separations, Singapore
Printed and bound in
Malaysia by Times Offset (M) Sdn Bhd

04 03 02 01 00 99   6 5 4 3 2 1

CONTENTS

IMPERIAL VERSUS METRIC

When using the patterns in this book, follow either the metric or the imperial measurements given, do not mix them, as they are not always exact equivalents.

Work in the system with which you are most familiar. Occasionally, however, you will need to do a quick conversion, so it is worth learning one or two equivalents. Most people know that a metre is a little more than a yard but fewer could tell you that a yard is about 90 centimetres and therefore, a foot is about 30 centimetres. A quick look at your tape measure will reassure you that an inch is 2.5 centimetres. Turning it the other way around, 10 centimetres is about 4 in., 20 is about 8 and 25 about 10 in.

Nevertheless here are a few exact conversions that may prove useful:

1in = 2.54cm	1cm = 0.39in
1foot = 30.48cm	25cm = 9.8in
1yard = 91.44cm	90cm = 35.37in
45in = 114.3cm	1m = 39.37in
48in = 121.9cm	115cm = 45.27in
60in = 152.4cm	150cm = 53in

Most rotary cutting equipment is marked in inches, although if you prefer to use the metric system, there are rotary cutting tools available. The grid is marked at intervals of 0.25cm. Seam allowances therefore have to be selected to fit with these markings, so the standard seam allowance using metric measurements is 0.75cm and this is used throughout the book. Make sure that your sewing machine is set up to do this if you do use metric tools (see page 12).

FROM TRADITION TO TEXTILE ART:
A Brief History of Patchwork & Quilting

Patchwork and quilting are familiar partners in the craft world but, though they've been together for thousands of years, each has its own separate history and retains its own characteristics. Both can be either functional or decorative – or both at once – and both have continually been reinterpreted and reinvented by succeeding generations. In conjunction, they form a unique craft – and one which has risen to the level of fine art, as shown in the examples displayed in the Quilt Gallery on pages 162 to 169.

HOW OLD IS QUILTING?

Traditions of quilting go back many centuries in many parts of the world but, since textiles are fragile, early survivals are few. The word "quilt" itself comes from the Latin "culcita", a mattress or cushion filled with something soft and warm (such as feathers, wool or hair) and used both for lying on and as a covering. Evidence of the existence of quilting goes back centuries before the Romans, though. Burial places (in which objects were preserved from the damaging effects of light, air, dirt and use) have yielded the finest finds. A small carved ivory figure, found in Egypt and believed to date from 3400BC, shows a King of Lower Egypt wrapped in a mantle – on which the carved decoration has all the characteristics of quilting and the pattern employs the same diamond or lozenge combinations that are still popular today. A funerary carpet, found in Russia on the floor of a chieftain's tomb and dated between 100BC and 200AD, is probably the oldest actual quilted item to have survived. One of the most beautiful and affecting survivals is an elegant quilted slipper, found in the rubbish dump of a Tibetan garrison on the Silk Road and thought to have been made between 750 and 860AD. It is from such rare and often damaged fragments that a tentative history of early quilting has to be constructed.

Certainly one of the most important uses for quilting in many early societies was in the construction of body armour. Strong, well-padded and well-quilted fabric made an effective defence against swords, spears and arrows. It was used by Chinese, Korean and Japanese armies, by the Rajputs in India and throughout Europe until well into the Middle Ages.

Although occasional surviving articles – such as some quilts found in Sicily which date from the end of the fourteenth century – give at least a little direct evidence of styles and techniques in use in particular periods and societies, it's only when we get well into the Middle Ages that there is sufficient written evidence for us to construct a coherent story. Even those written records, though, only tell a part of that story – the part referring to the rich – because the references to quilts and quilting occur mostly in the inventories and household accounts of upper-class families. Still, it's reasonable to suppose that the women from poorer families, who actually made the quilts to which those records refer, would also have used their skills at home – so that quilts and quilted clothing would have been used in the poorest as well as in the richest homes.

WHAT ABOUT PATCHWORK?

There are even fewer surviving examples of patchwork – precisely because it was a "make do and mend" recycling technique, using pieces most of which would already have had hard wear in some other form. Until well into the seventeenth century, most fabric was produced at home by individual households, who first grew the plants, then spun the threads and finally wove the fabrics. These were valuable commodities and were only discarded when their last possible use had been exhausted. That "last possible use" was often in a patchwork.

QUILTING IN THE BRITISH ISLES

Good examples of British quilting survive from at least as early as the beginning of the eighteenth century. These survivals are often pieces of clothing, such as petticoats or caps, though quilted bedcovers also exist. Not that English patchwork was necessarily quilted. Often it was just lined – and, as a result, less sturdy and durable.

Patchwork and quilting were common occupations through most of society, right up until the time when manufactured clothing and bedcoverings became generally available. Then they became associated with the poor, who couldn't afford to buy manufactured, ready-made goods. That association between patchwork and poverty lasted until changing social patterns after World War II (with more and more women going out to work) dramatically affected the whole role of patchwork and quilting.

The British Regions

Certain areas of the British Isles had particularly strong patchwork and quilting traditions. They produced their own distinctive piecing and quilting styles and are the places where the popularity of patchwork and quilting has been least affected by the social changes of this century. The most outstanding examples are Wales and the North Country (Northumberland, Durham and, to an extent, Cumbria). Elaborate and closely worked quilting in traditional patterns is characteristic of both regions.

The quilts most typical of the North Country are made from a single piece of cloth, the pattern being produced entirely by the quilting design. You will find them described as "North Country quilts" or "Durham quilts" or "wholecloth quilts" (see page 40).

The quilts typical of Wales feature large patchwork designs pieced from rich and darkly colored woollen fabrics. The results are frequently bold, vigorous and vividly graphic. In the past, the batting for these quilts was often sheep's wool or recycled blankets.

PATCHWORKING AND QUILTING GO WEST

In America, patchwork and quilting have been more or less continuously part of the social scene, particularly in rural areas, since settlement days. For women who were often living in isolated places and moving from one place to another, patchwork and quilting were simultaneously a survival tool, a social outlet and almost the only available form of creative expression. They were a social outlet because co-operation on the assembly and quilting of large items was an excuse for far-flung neighbours to come together for some gossip, fun and mutual sympathy as they plied their needles.

The characteristic American method of working in blocks almost certainly developed for simple practical reasons. Blocks were easy to carry when the family moved and they could be picked up and worked on at odd times by people either on the move or living in confined spaces. Only when all the required blocks were completed was it necessary to find the space to assemble and complete them by adding batting and quilting.

THE AMERICAN REGIONS

Of course, settlers from different countries took the skills and styles of their localities with them; characteristics that are still apparent in the work done today. The quilts of the Pennsylvanian Deutsch (often mis-named "Dutch"), for example, still retain a strong flavour of their German past, using appliquéd folk motifs similar to those painted on their furniture and houses.

THE PRESENT BOOM: FROM FOLK ART TO FINE ART

It is American rather than British quilting which has had such an enormous influence in recent years all around the world, particularly in places such as Australia and Japan. That is certainly true of contemporary quilts made in traditional styles. It is even more true of non-traditional quilts. In the 1970s, students of American folk crafts began to collect traditional patchwork quilts. They didn't just collect them, they hung them on walls and asked people to admire and appreciate them at least in part for their resemblance to certain modern paintings. (Of course, the quilts were made long before the paintings.) When textile artists, too, began to take an interest in quilts and to make them for exhibition on walls rather than for utility on beds, "quilt art" was born.

WHAT IS QUILTING FOR?

There are as many reasons to make quilts as there are people who make them. They can simply be something to keep somebody warm. They can be loving copies of old quilts, celebrating the past, or innovative interpretations of them, both as a tribute to past skills and as a display of present achievements. They can express a point of view, whether angry or sad, satirical or light-hearted. They can say things about the maker and her or his life which it simply isn't possible to say in any other way. They can play with pattern and texture for the sheer pleasure of the exercise and the beauty of the result.

Why is it still so popular? Perhaps just because of that many-sidedness, its ability to be, if not all things to all people, then at least something important to just about everyone. Certainly patchwork quilting is one of the few areas of expression which has the power to unite and to satisfy both those who are in love with the useful and those who are in love with the beautiful, those who are in love with the past and those who look to the future. Long may it continue to do so.

EQUIPMENT AND MATERIALS

WHAT DO YOU NEED?

If you've got fabric, scissors, pins, needles, thread, a ruler and some cardboard or plastic for templates, you can get started on a hand-sewn patchwork. To quilt your patchwork, all you need is some fabric to back it with and some batting to place between the top and the backing. It's as simple as that.

On the other hand, today we do have an array of tools and equipment to choose from and it's sometimes difficult to tell the useful from the gimmicky. The following is a guide to a range of tools, equipment and materials which have proved their worth to many patchwork quilters.

SCISSORS

Scissors are so important it's worth getting different scissors for specific purposes. These are the most useful:

Large fabric scissors: Those with spring-loaded handles are easy to use and recommended by people with hand or wrist problems.

Small, fine-pointed scissors: For snipping machine threads, trimming corners and other small jobs.

Round-pointed paper scissors: For cutting cardboard, paper and template plastic.

ROTARY CUTTER AND SELF-HEALING MAT

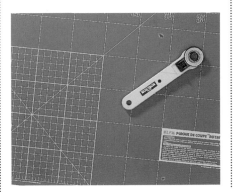

The disc blade of the rotary cutter is good for cutting through several thicknesses of fabric in an unbroken line without needing to lift the fabric.

The mat on which you cut absorbs the action of the blade, making a clean cut. It is marked in squares to enable you to measure your patches and cut them to exactly the right size. Angled lines enable you to cut various sorts of triangles. Choose a mat of suitable size to fit easily on your table, without overlapping it. A good average-sized mat is 17 x 23in. Some mats are also marked on the reverse in metric units.

RULERS

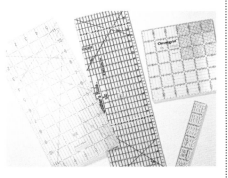

For use with the rotary cutter you need a special ruler, made of heavy-duty acrylic, which is at least as long as the mat is wide. There's a wide range of rulers for various purposes, from small, 6in rulers to large 24in ones, and these are available in several widths. Most are marked in metric or imperial squares.

Two particularly useful rulers for drafting blocks are:
- a 12½in square ruler for checking sizes of finished 12in blocks and for squaring up blocks of smaller sizes
- a transparent ruler 24 x 2in which includes markings down to ⅛in.

PINS

Ordinary dressmaker's pins are fine for small patches. Use the longer, glass-headed pins for larger patches and for pinning quilts together. Some extra long, fine glass-headed pins are useful for pinning through several layers. Flat-headed (or flower-headed) pins are ideal for pinning patches which are to be machine-sewn, as the needle can run over them without damage.

SAFETY PINS

These can be used instead of basting stitches to secure the quilt sandwich prior to quilting.

NEEDLES

You need general purpose needles in a variety of sizes for basting and for hand-sewing patches together. You also need special needles for hand-quilting. These are called "betweens" and are short but quite fine, with a large enough eye to accommodate quilting thread. Betweens come in sizes from about 5 to 12, 12 being the smallest and finest. For general purposes, use size 9 or 10 betweens. For thicker items, choose size 7 or 8. For very fine small stitches, 11 or 12 betweens are available, although these can be quite difficult to thread.

THREADS

Whether you are hand- or machine-piecing, it's important to use good quality threads which will stand up to wear and tear. Cheap threads may disintegrate in the seams and cause your patchwork to come apart. Poor quality, or unsuitable threads, may also break or snag in the sewing machine.

Invisible thread, also known as "monofilament", can be useful for machine-quilting. It can be used where you want a quilted contour but don't want the quilting stitches to show, to quilt along the seam lines of pieced patchwork ("in-the-ditch") or simply where you don't want to keep changing the color of the spool.

For hand-quilting, use special quilting threads which are strong, thick and hard-wearing. They come in a wide range of colours that you can either match to the fabrics in your project or use as a contrast.

BEESWAX

Running a thread through a block of beeswax before sewing strengthened it and made it easier to pull through fabric. Modern quilting threads don't need this treatment, but some people still prefer to do it and most quilting suppliers stock beeswax.

SEAM RIPPER

We all make mistakes and this is the quickest and easiest tool for taking out both hand and machine stitches.

THIMBLES

Essential for hand-quilting, the best one for pushing the needle through the quilt sandwich has a small ridge around the crown, which prevents the needle from slipping. There are also finger-guards (including some made of leather) for protecting the finger that is used underneath the quilt.

HOOPS AND FRAMES

Floor-standing frames offer the largest area for quilting large quilts and some can be tilted to make the quilt surface easier to reach (see page 36 for how to use a frame). If you don't have space for a stand, there are excellent self-assembly frames, usually sold as kits. These consist of a series of tubular plastic poles which are very light and which lock together to make a frame of whatever length and width you need. Some of them can be fitted with legs to make the frame floor-standing. They can easily be disassembled and stored when not in use.

A popular and convenient alternative to working in a frame is to use a hoop. Quilting hoops are stronger and more solid than embroidery (or tambour) hoops and are available in various sizes, oval or round.

For machine-quilting, plastic half-hoops, in large or small sizes, grip the quilt surface and enable you to move the quilt under the needle easily.

MARKERS AND ERASERS

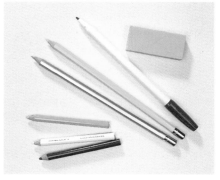

You need markers for drawing around templates, for marking quilt tops ready for quilting and for making labels to go on the backs of quilts.

In choosing a marker for the top of a quilt, consider which is most suitable for the fabric and colours you're using. For example, if the fabrics, or some of them, aren't washable, you must use a marker which can be removed without water, for example by rubbing or using a dry eraser. There's a wide range of markers to choose from, including:

Soft lead pencils, 2B for example, make good clear lines without dragging or distortion of the fabric. The marks can be rubbed off easily with a non-smudge fabric eraser.

Quilters' silver pencils can be sharpened to make a fine point and are good for marking both light and dark fabrics. Like ordinary lead pencils, they can be removed with a fabric eraser.

Vanishing marking pens make a line which fades away after a few hours. One possible disadvantage is that these pens are thought by some to rot or weaken fabrics over a period of time.

Water-erasable pens make a mark like blue felt pen. The line tends to be rather thick, though, making it difficult to maintain straight quilting lines. These pens should always be tested on fabric before use, to make sure that the marks will come out when washed. Care is needed during use because exposure to certain conditions, such as sunlight and heat, can cause them to become permanent. On the other hand, damp conditions may cause them to fade before you finish the quilting.

Soapstone pencils make clear marks on most fabrics and are easily washed out.

Soap slivers are the quilter's traditional stand-by. The soap must be hard and dry before it is pared to a sharp edge. It's easy to see on darker fabrics and, of course, will wash out completely.

Hera markers (the traditional Japanese method of marking quilts) are small, wedge-shaped tools with a sharp edge that make a clearly visible line when run over the fabric. The mark is short-lived, so the hera is most suitable for small items or for quilting patterns which you can mark a little at a time.

Tailor's chalk wheel markers are easy to use and the marks can be brushed off. White chalk is available for use on dark fabric, colours for lighter fabric. As with the hera, this method is most suitable for small items or patterns which you can mark as you go.

White chinagraph pencils are useful for darker fabrics, while blue ones can be used on light fabrics. They are best used where a very fine line is not needed. It's also a good idea to test the blue ones on light fabrics to make sure that the color can be rubbed or washed away.

Dressmakers' carbon provides a very easy way of transferring quilting patterns to fabric but care is needed as the lines can be difficult to remove from some fabrics. Test before using.

Pigma pens are used for making permanent labels or for writing on quilts. They are filled with indelible ink and are available in several colours.

TEMPLATES AND TEMPLATE KITS

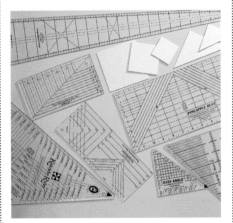

Commercially-produced templates, particularly those made of strong clear plastic, are accurate and can be used indefinitely without wearing out. Sets containing all the different templates needed to make particular block patterns are very useful, particularly if you want to make several repeats of a block. There are also many templates for use with a rotary cutter, some of which are marked to enable you to cut triangles, circles and other shapes. These include the following:

• Equilateral triangle (60º);
• Right-angled triangle;
• Birangle™, for cutting bias rectangles;
• Pineapple ruler, for accurately cutting pieces for the traditional pineapple block;
• Circle wedge ruler (90º) for making circles and fans;
• Kaleidoscope ruler to make the triangles for kaleidoscope blocks;
• Scrap saver to cut half and quarter square triangles out of odd pieces for making scrap quilts.

Cardboard and Template Plastic

To make your own templates, you need either cardboard or template plastic.

Use the strongest cardboard you can find. The best choice is the heavy mounting board sold in artist's supplies shops. To cut it, use a sharp craft knife and a metal ruler.

Template plastic is sold in sheets or rolls, the sheets being easier to handle. It can easily be cut with scissors and has one rough surface to hold pencil marks. As the plastic is transparent, it is possible to position the templates over particular parts of a patterned fabric.

EQUIPMENT FOR DRAFTING AND DESIGN

Art shops supply gridded paper, tracing paper and also isometric paper, which is marked in triangles and is useful for drawing out diamond and hexagonal patterns, such as "Tumbling Blocks" or "Grandmother's Garden".

A set of good quality coloured pencils and felt pens is useful for working out color combinations.

A pair of hinged mirrors is ideal for working out pattern repeats and kaleidoscope effects. They can be bought ready-made but you can easily make your own from two mirror-tiles joined with masking tape.

Compass

The best and most useful compass can be fitted with an extending arm, making it possible to draw extra-large circles and arcs.

Protractor

This allows you to measure angles and to draft triangles.

Set-square

To measure accurate right angles.

Viewers

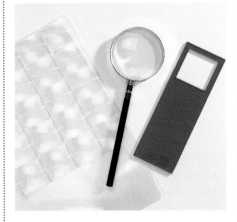

These tools help you work out the patterning of your quilt:

The Ruby Beholder® or Value Finder is a red coloured lens which, when you look through it, eliminates color from fabrics. You can then identify light, medium and dark values and arrange fabrics accordingly.

A reducing glass is the opposite of a magnifying glass. Look through this to see how your block or quilt will look when viewed from a distance. Alternatively, use the wrong end of binoculars or buy the spy glass for a door from a builders' supply store.

Multi-image Lens: Look through this to see how one block will look when multiplied. Most multi-image lenses allow you to see twenty-five repeated images.

Light Box

This is a closed box with a Plexiglas top and a bulb inside. When lit, place pattern and fabric over the glass and the pattern will become visible on the fabric. You can then trace the pattern onto the fabric. This is particularly useful for transferring quilting patterns onto darker fabrics. A light box is an expensive piece of equipment to buy but you can improvise one for yourself.

Place a piece of Plexiglas, the edges safely covered with masking tape, on two supports, such as piles of books. Make sure that it is steady and leave enough space between the supports to put a small lamp under the glass, but do not leave it there for too long or the glass will become very hot.

EQUIPMENT FOR FOUNDATION PIECING
A popular method of piecing involves stitching onto a marked background, the "foundation" (see pages 120 to 127). You can either stitch onto a muslin backing on which you've marked the stitching lines, or use special paper which can be drawn on, stitched on, then removed by tearing it away from the stitches.

Freezer Paper
This thick, white paper is slightly adhesive when applied to fabric with a hot iron but easily peels off when no longer needed. It can be used for appliqué or for making the paper templates for English patchwork.

Fusible Webbing
This has become a very popular method of appliqué. The fusible webbing comes on sheets of paper which can be drawn on and cut to any shape or size. The rough side is placed on the fabric and pressed with a hot iron. When the paper is removed, a fine layer of adhesive is left on the fabric which can then be ironed onto a background. Although the fusible webbing bonds the fabrics together very firmly, it's common to complete the appliqué by sewing around the outlines of the shapes, either with blanket stitch or satin stitch, to seal the edges.

The disadvantage of fusible webbing is that it stiffens the fabrics to which it is applied, making it unsuitable for hand-quilting.

SEWING MACHINES
Except for dedicated hand-piecers, a sewing machine is an indispensable item of equipment. But it doesn't have to be a sophisticated model. Any machine which can produce straight, even stitching is adequate for making basic patchwork. The following guidelines will help you get the best from your machine:
• Regular servicing by a specialist sewing machine mechanic will give even an old and well-used machine a new lease of life. Look in Yellow Pages or ask in a local fabric shop for a suitable specialist.
• Check the manufacturer's instructions for basic maintenance you can carry out yourself. (Oiling it and tightening its screws, for example.)
• Most important of all, regularly remove the deposits of lint and dust which quickly build up under and around the bobbin case, especially if you are using woollen fabrics. (This is another situation where a seam ripper is very handy. Use the sharp point to remove any thick deposits, then a small brush for the dust.)

Modern machines offer many features which are useful to the quiltmaker. If cost is a consideration, it's particularly important to have a clear idea of what you want the machine to do, then to research the possibilities within your price range.

The following features are generally useful to the average quiltmaker:

Stitch Reverse Function
This is useful for finishing seams so that they won't unravel at the end.

Swing Needle Function
This is used for machine appliqué and over-sewing seams.

Changeable Feet

Walking or even-feed foot: An attachment for straight line machine-quilting that feeds the top and bottom fabrics of a quilt sandwich through evenly.

Darning foot: Use this attachment for free-motion machine-quilting patterns.

Embroidery foot: Use this for surface embellishment of your fabrics.

Feed Dog Cover Plate
This or a device for dropping the feed dogs is necessary for machine-quilting.

Adjustability
Free-motion machine quilting is easier if you are be able to adjust your machine so that the footplate is flush with the table-top. This allows you to move the quilt around smoothly. Some machines have a special table with the necessary well to drop it into. The alternative is to make or buy an extension which can be fitted to the machine.

Computerized Machines
These offer an even wider range of functions. If you're considering investing in one of these, try to be realistic about the features you really need and would use. There's no point in spending a large sum of money on a piece of equipment you won't fully use. Check out the demonstrations by manufacturers at the major quilt shows.

AMERICAN BLOCK PIECING

A block is a square unit of pattern made up of smaller pieces. These pieces are first stitched into blocks, then joined to form the patchwork top. In American Block Piecing, the patches that make up the block are placed right sides together and sewn together with a plain running stitch. This is different from English Piecing (see pages 44 to 45), where the patches are first basted over paper templates, then joined by overstitching.

1 First choose your block, then make the necessary templates. To make your own templates, draw out the block full size and trace out the shapes you need onto cardboard or template plastic. Before you cut out the templates, add ¼in/0.75cm for the seam allowance. If you're using triangles, measure ¼in/0.75cm from the straight edges, then extend the lines beyond the point until they meet. (See pages 68 to 71 for more information on drafting.)

Tip *When cutting patches, align one edge of the template with the straight grain of the fabric. Where possible, have the straight grain on the outer edge of the patch (diagram 1).*

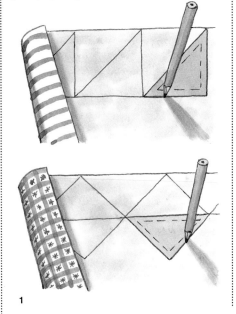

1

2 Choose your fabrics and decide where to place them in your block. Draw around the templates onto the back of the fabric, using a 2B pencil or other marker. Cut out carefully.

3 Place the fabric patches right sides together and stitch a ¼in/0.75cm seam. If you're hand-stitching, mark the seam allowance around each patch, then sew along the pencil lines. If you're machine-stitching, you can either add the pencil lines and sew along those, or set your sewing machine to sew an exact ¼in/0.75cm seam.

Seam Allowance on Machine

If your sewing machine does not have a ¼in/0.75cm guideline marked on the throat plate or a special foot, the edge of which is exactly ¼in from the needle, you can buy a small magnetic plate which can be attached to the throat plate to act as a guide. But **beware**: this must not be used on computerized sewing machines.

To make your own guide, fold a piece of fabric in two and iron the fold. Place it under the needle so that the folded edge is exactly ¼in or 0.75cm away from the needle. Check by making a line of stitching and measuring the seam. When you're satisfied that it's accurate, place a piece of masking tape along the throat cover to mark the line where the edge of the fabric should be placed to stitch the seam.

Tip *If you build up three or four layers of tape, it will form a slight "buffer", which will ensure that the edge of the fabric doesn't move off the line as you stitch.*

ORDER OF PIECING WITHIN A BLOCK

In working out the order in which to piece the units within a block, try to avoid sewing into awkward angles, known as "setting-in" (see opposite).

Most blocks can be broken down into a series of units which can be joined in straight rows (diagram 2a to c).

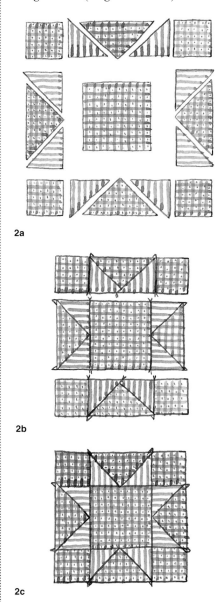

2a

2b

2c

DIRECTION OF PRESSED SEAMS

You can either press seams open or to one side and there are advantages and disadvantages in both methods. Pressing them to one side is quicker and gives a stronger seam because there is less stress on the stitches. The disadvantage is that where a dark and a light fabric meet you must remember to press the lighter fabric towards the darker or the dark fabric may show through on the quilt surface. It also means that you have an extra layer of fabric to stitch through if you are hand-quilting, which may be a disadvantage if the quilting pattern crosses over the seams.

Opening the seams takes a little longer but makes it easier to get a good, crisp seam line and makes joining seams easier. It's also useful if you're outline quilting, because the seam allowance makes a slight ridge which you can use as a quilting guide, avoiding the need to mark quilting lines first.

Some people prefer not to iron their seams during construction of the block and it is possible simply to "finger press" them (i.e. pressing firmly between your fingers.)

If you prefer to iron as you go, press lightly to avoid distorting the fabric.

MATCHING SEAMS

When joining the units of the block, the seams should match exactly. To do this, first match the seams and pin them together. Put the pin vertically into the point where they meet so that the two seams don't slide apart. Pin the rest of the seam, easing gently to fit.

SETTING-IN SEAMS

This is necessary when three seams meet, for example in piecing hexagons or diamonds.

1   Before you begin sewing, make a dot exactly ¼in/0.75cm from the end of each seam. Join the first two patches, sewing from the opposite end of the seam from the setting-in point but stop exactly on the dot (diagram 3a).

2   Take a backstitch to anchor the thread, then cut it off. Add the third patch to the second patch, again sewing exactly to the dot and anchoring the thread (diagram 3b).

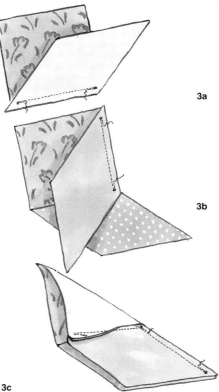

3a

3b

3c

3   Pivot the third patch to line up with the first patch and sew from dot to dot (diagram 3c). The important point in setting-in patches is not to sew into the seam allowance.

CURVED SEAMS

Sewing curved seams accurately needs practice. It's wise to make a few sample blocks to master the technique. The "Drunkard's Path" block is a good starting point (diagram 4). Note that in the following method pins are avoided because they make it more difficult to ease the layers as you sew.

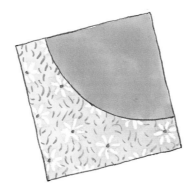

4

1   Using templates which include seam allowance, cut patches.

2   Clip the concave curve at intervals of about 1½in/4cm, taking care not to snip beyond the seam allowance.

3   Line up the outer edges, which are the straight side of the block, and position the starting edges of the two pieces under the machine with the concave curve on top. If possible, reduce the speed on your machine. Sew carefully, easing the two edges together and trying to ensure that the needle is always exactly ¼in/0.75cm from the edge of the patches (diagram 5).

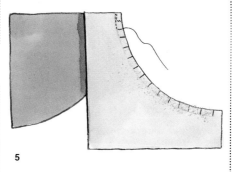

5

Tip   If you have a binding foot, which gives a clear view of the space between the needle and the edge of the fabric, this is a useful aid.

4   Use your seam ripper or scissors to ease the edges together. Only stitch a short distance, then stop with the needle in the fabric, lift the presser foot and line up the next section, gently easing the clipped curve and watching that ¼in/0.75cm seam allowance (diagram 6).

6

Crazy Anne At Home

THE FOLLOWING PROJECT GUIDES YOU THROUGH THE BASICS OF MAKING AMERICAN BLOCK PATCHWORK. IT USES A TRADITIONAL FIVE-PATCH BLOCK, "CRAZY ANNE", WHICH IS EASILY PIECED BUT PRODUCES INTERESTING SECONDARY PATTERNS WHEN SEVERAL BLOCKS ARE PLACED SIDE BY SIDE. TEMPLATES SHOWN ARE FOR A 12IN/30CM BLOCK AND THERE ARE FOUR BLOCKS IN THE QUILT. IF YOU WANT TO MAKE A LARGER ITEM, SUCH AS A BED QUILT OR THROW, SIMPLY MAKE MORE BLOCKS. TWELVE BLOCKS, I.E. FOUR ROWS OF THREE BLOCKS, MAKE A GOOD LAP QUILT.

Quilt size: 30 x 30in/60 x 60cm

Materials

All fabrics used in the patchwork top are 45in/115cm wide.
- ▣ Template plastic or thin cardboard
- ▣ Block fabric 1: cream ¼yard/23cm
- ▣ Block fabric 2: dark green ¼yard/23cm
- ▣ Block fabric 3: medium green ¼yard/23cm
- ▣ Block fabric 4: light brown ⅜yard/34cm
- ▣ Block fabric 5: red ¼yard/23cm

- ▣ Border fabric: ½yard/45cm – either repeat block fabric 1 or choose a different one which tones with your block fabrics
- ▣ Backing fabric: 32 x 32in/81 x 81cm – use plain muslin or some other cotton fabric which tones with the front of your quilt
- ▣ Batting: 2oz. polyester, 32 x 32in/81 x 81cm
- ▣ Size 8 pearl cotton in a coordinating color

CUTTING

The Crazy Anne block is made up of
four different templates and five fabric
colours. The templates given on page 18
include seam allowance of
¼in/0.75cm. Trace them onto template
plastic or cardboard and cut them out.

1   Using Template A, cut: 16 patches
in fabric 1; 16 patches in fabric 2.
(Note: Template A must always be used
facing the same way up.)

2   Using Template B, cut: 16
patches in fabric 4.

3   Using Template C, cut: 32
patches in fabric 3.

4   Using Template D, cut: 20
patches in fabric 5.

STITCHING

1   First assemble the individual
blocks by joining the pieces. When
deciding on the order in which to
piece the component parts of a block,
the aim is always to be able to stitch in
straight lines. Follow the order shown
in diagrams 1a to 1d.

2   As you assemble the units of
each block, either press seams open or
press them to one side. If you choose to
press them to one side, make sure that
where a dark and a light fabric are
joined, you press towards the dark side.
You can either finger-press or use light
pressure with an iron. Don't iron too
firmly at this stage in case you distort
the fabrics.

3   When you've stitched the four
blocks together, check the
measurements. They should each
measure 12½in/32cm square.

4   Following the quilt assembly
plan, stitch them together in two pairs,
then stitch the two pairs together, being
careful to match the seams.

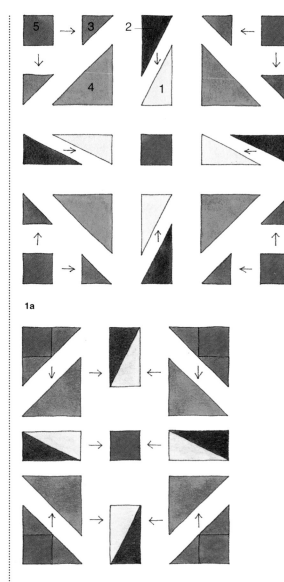

1a

1b

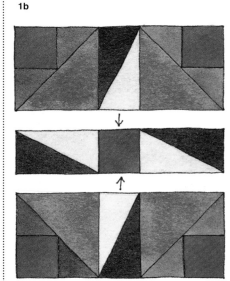

1c

1d

ADDING BORDERS

1   From the border fabric, cut four pieces measuring exactly 24½in/62cm long by 4in/10cm wide.

2   From fabric 5, cut four squares measuring 4 x 4in/10 x 10cm.

3   Now place one 24½in/62cm strip, right sides together, along one side of the pieced top. Pin, easing to fit as necessary, and stitch using a ¼in/0.75cm seam.

4   Add another 24½in/62cm strip to the opposite edge (diagram 2).

2

5   Now add one of the squares to each end of the two remaining strips, pin them to the two remaining sides so that the seams match, and sew as before (diagram 3).

3

FINISHING

The "bagging-out" method is used here, which is simpler than adding bindings and therefore suitable for a first quilt.

1   Work on a flat surface big enough to take the whole quilt. Gently press the pieced top. Lay out first the batting, then the backing, right side **up**, and finally the pieced quilt top right side **down**. Pin all layers together using large glass-headed pins or flat-headed "flower" pins.

2   Trim the backing and batting even with the pieced top.

3   Stitch all three layers together using a ½in/1.5cm seam and leaving an opening of about 12in/30cm on the fourth side. Remove pins. Trim seams to ⅜in/1cm (diagram 4).

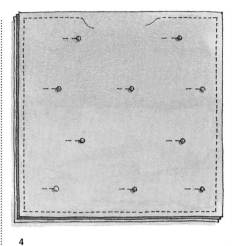

4

4   Turn right side out. Press the seams and close the opening with small slipstitches.

5   Pin the layers together securely. Using the pearl cotton, make ties at all the seam intersections as described on page 38. Machine around the sides close to the edge.

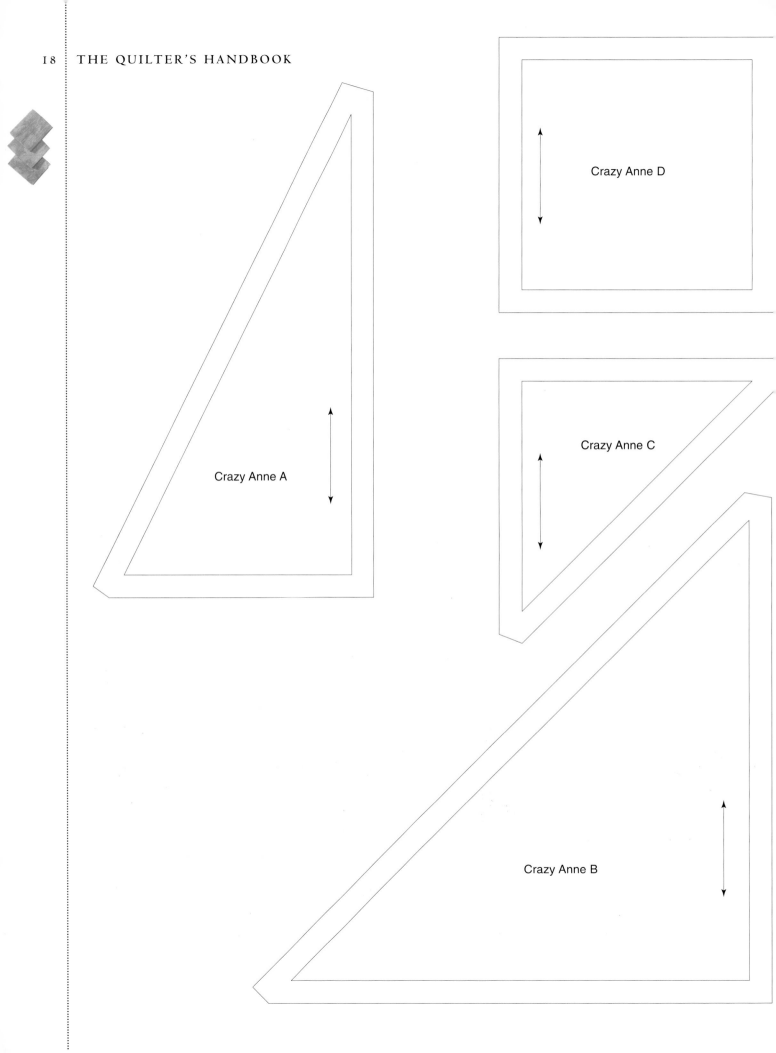

Crazy Anne A

Crazy Anne B

Crazy Anne C

Crazy Anne D

QUILT LAYOUT AND ASSEMBLY

BLOCK ARRANGEMENT

The previous quilt demonstrated the secondary designs which fabric choice within the block can produce. This was shown with a basic straight setting of the blocks (see below). There are, however, a variety of other arrangement options for assembling the blocks into a patchwork top.

Straight Setting

For this the blocks are arranged side by side in rows (diagram 1). Lay them out on a bed or on the floor and move them around until they are arranged as you want them. Some block patterns produce interesting effects when rotated, so it's worth spending some time trying out various possibilities.

On-Point Setting

In this arrangement, the blocks are arranged diagonally across the quilt. For this it's necessary to add half-blocks or triangles to complete the top (diagram 2). Cut the triangles so that the side that will be on the quilt edge will be on the straight grain (diagram 2a).

For either arrangement, pin the blocks together in rows and sew one row at a time (diagram 3). Now carefully pin the first row to the second one, making sure that the seams match. Sew together and add the remaining rows, one at a time, in the same way (diagram 4).

SASHINGS OR DIVIDERS

Sashings or dividers are vertical and horizontal strips between the blocks which create a lattice effect. They can be plain (diagram 5), or squares in a contrasting fabric can be added where the strips meet to create "sashing squares" or "posts" (diagram 6). Sashing is particularly appropriate in a sampler quilt where you want the individual blocks to stand out.

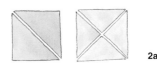

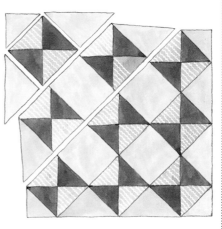

1

2a

2

3

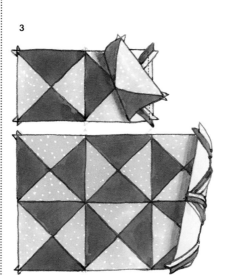

4

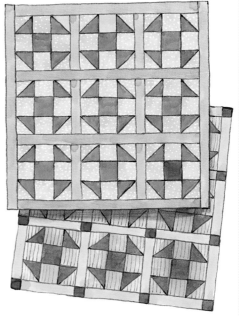

5

6

TO ADD PLAIN SASHINGS
(i.e. without the posts)

The horizontal sashings will all be the same width as the quilt. You'll need one for the top, one for the bottom and enough to divide the rows. For the vertical sashings, you will need two which measure the depth of the quilt once the horizontal sashings have all been added and shorter sashings the depth of the individual blocks – enough to divide the blocks.

1 Decide on the width of the border, which will be the width of the sashings. Remember to add seam allowances.

2 Work out how many short vertical sashings you need, depending on the number of blocks in the quilt.

3 Cut the required number of strips the same length as the blocks (e.g. 12½in/31.5cm) and arrange these between the blocks.

4 Take the lefthand block in the first row and place a sashing strip over the righthand edge, right sides together and matching raw edges. Stitch the seam and press to one side away from the sashing (diagram 7).

5 Take the next block and place over the sashing strip just attached, right sides together and matching raw edges. Stitch and press the seam away from the sashing strip. Continue in this way until all the blocks in a row are joined. Repeat with the other rows.

6 Measure the rows and cut sashing strips of that length. You will need one more than the number of rows in the patchwork. Sew the rows together with the sashings between them as before.

7 Stitch horizontal sashings to the top and bottom of the quilt.

7

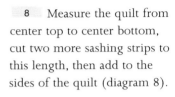

8

9

10

11

8 Measure the quilt from center top to center bottom, cut two more sashing strips to this length, then add to the sides of the quilt (diagram 8).

TO ADD SASHINGS WITH POSTS

You will need sashing strips of the same width and length to join all the blocks plus to add a border around all four sides, as well as squares to join each sashing strip (diagram 9).

1 Decide on the width of the sashing.

2 Work out how many joining and side sashing strips you need.

3 Cut this number of strips the same size as the blocks.

4 Join blocks in rows with sashing strips between them and one at each end (diagram 10).

5 Cut squares exactly the same size as the width of the sashings (e.g. if the strips are 3½in/9cm wide, cut squares 3½ x 3½in/9 x 9cm).

6 Join squares and sashing strips, beginning and ending with a square each time (diagram 11).

7 Sew the rows of blocks together with strips between them, taking care to match the seams at each join.

8 Complete by adding a row of sashing strips and squares to the top and bottom of the patchwork.

BORDERS

Borders can be plain or with corner posts. Plain borders can be straight or mitered at the corners (diagram 1).

1

You can add more than one border to a patchwork and vary the widths and colours, as shown in "Rail Fence" on page 83.

To determine the length of the borders, measure the quilt through the center. This is because any inaccuracies in the piecing of the blocks will distort the measurements at the edges, perhaps giving two different measurements. If the border is cut to the center length it's easy to adjust and ease the quilt edges to fit it. This will give a flat, rather than a wavy edge, to the quilt.

Plain Borders

1   Decide on the width of the borders, adding seam allowances. This is the width to cut strips.

2   Measure the length of the quilt from center top to center bottom (diagram 2).

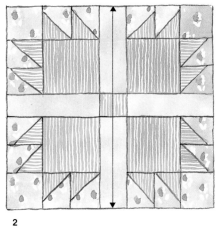

2

3   Cut two strips of this length. If necessary, join strips to achieve the correct length.

Tip   *Conceal the joins in the strips by using an angled seam (diagram 3).*

3

4   Pin the strips, right sides together, to the sides of the quilt. To get a good fit, find the center of the quilt and the center of the border and pin. Ease the top to fit the borders and sew together using ¼in/0.75cm seam.

5   Measure the width of the quilt, including the newly added borders, from center side to center side and cut strips of this length. Stitch to the top and bottom of the quilt, pinning and easing as before.

Borders with Corner Posts

1   Follow step 1 above.

2   Measure the width of the quilt and cut two strips to these measurements. Repeat for the length.

3   Stitch one strip to the top and one to the bottom of the quilt, as described above.

4   In contrasting fabric, cut four squares the same width as the border. Add one square to each end of the remaining two strips.

5   Pin one strip to each side of the quilt, right sides together, matching the seams, then sew together (diagram 4).

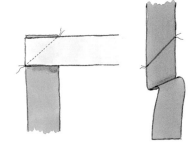

4

Mitered Borders

For a mitered border, the border strips are joined with a diagonal seam, resembling a picture frame.

1   Decide on the width of the borders, adding seam allowances.

2   Measure the length and width of the patchwork top.

3   Cut border strips to match these measurements **plus** twice the width of the border including seam allowances. For example, if the patchwork measures 48 x 48in/122 x 122cm and the desired width of the border is 3½in/9cm, border strips should be cut 55in/140cm long.

4   Pin the borders, right sides together, to all four sides, leaving an even amount of excess at each end.

5 Stitch to within ¼in/0.75cm of each end. Backstitch to secure the end of the seam. Press the seams towards the border.

6 Lay the patchwork top on a flat surface and lay the border strips one on top of the other (diagram 5).

5

7 Carefully turn under the top strip at an a 45-degree angle and pin in place (diagram 6).

6

8 Slipstitch the top strip to the bottom strip and trim away excess fabric from underneath. Press neatly (diagram 7).

7

ASSEMBLING

In order to make a patchwork top into a wallhanging, coverlet or quilt, it will need to be backed and/or padded. The backing provides strength and hides the seams of the piecing. The batting adds loft (i.e. thickness) and warmth.

BATTING

It's important to choose batting which is right for your project. Here are some basic guidelines.

Polyester

The cheapest and most easily available is polyester, which is usually sold in two weights: 2oz and 4oz. For most purposes, the 2oz weight is a good choice, being easy to quilt through and washable. The 4oz weight makes a thicker quilt sandwich, so it's harder to quilt through and more suitable for large items that don't need fine quilting or are being tied rather than quilted. An advantage of polyester is that it won't move or bunch up even if you quilt it quite sparingly. It is sold in bed-size pieces ready-cut or off the bolt.

A disadvantage of polyester is the risk of "bearding". Bearding is when the polyester fibers travel up through the quilt top and appear on the surface as a fuzzy layer. This spoils the look of the quilt and reduces its lifespan. Avoid this by buying good-quality polyester and always check with the retailer that the brand you're buying is tested against bearding.

A very useful version of polyester batting is needlepunched during manu-facture, which makes it firm and unlikely to beard. It's excellent for any quilt or clothing where a firm "low loft" finish is wanted, i.e. with only thin padding.

Polyester batting is washable.

Cotton

The alternative to polyester is cotton. It gives a firmer and more solid finish, however, some versions do need to be quilted at small intervals to anchor them and to stop them from bunching up. To achieve the look, feel and drape of a traditional quilt, cotton batting is certainly the best choice. Cotton battings are also often sold as complete "batts", ready-cut to bed quilt size. Most cotton battings sold today are pre-shrunk and washable but it's always wise to check before you buy.

Wool

Wool batting has become very popular because of its warmth and ease of quilting. Modern versions are light in weight and not given to "bearding". Most of them are machine-washable but must be dried flat to avoid distortion. There are several brands of ready-cut, bed-sized batting available, although they are significantly more expensive than polyester or cotton battings.

ADDING BACKING AND BATTING

To add a backing only, cut a piece of backing the same size as the patchwork top and simply "bag out" as described on page 17.

If you are going to quilt the piece, you will probably need to add batting as well as backing. Cut the pieces of batting and backing 2in/5cm wider all around than the quilt top. For a large quilt you may have to join the backing and/or the batting.

If the backing is joined, press the seams open. Press the backing well.

To join batting, place the edges together without overlapping and herringbone-stitch them together.

To prepare and quilt the three layers see pages 36 to 41.

FINISHING

There are various ways in which you can finish the edges of your quilt.

Turning In or "Butting" the Edges

This is the way in which most traditional British quilts were finished and it's still a simple and effective method. The quilt edges are turned under to meet, then slip-stitched together. Make sure to turn the quilt top over the batting first, then turn the backing onto it (diagram 1).

1

Folding Backing Fabric to Front

One of the easiest ways to finish the edges is to bring the backing fabric over the front of the quilt. Turn it under so that it shows evenly all around, then pin, press and baste into position (diagram 2).

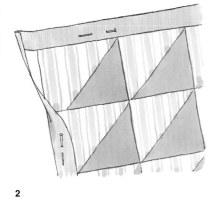

2

Attach it to the front with invisible hemstitches.

Binding

This is the method most often used on American quilts and it has become generally popular. Measure the width and length of your quilt and cut 3in/8cm wide strips of fabric on the straight grain (two for the length and two for the width), adding enough for a turning at the end of each strip. Fold each strip in half with the wrong sides together and press. Stitch the strips to the top and bottom of the quilt, right sides together, aligning raw edges. Turn each strip to the back, press and hemstitch down. Repeat for each side of the quilt, neatening the ends (diagrams 3a to c).

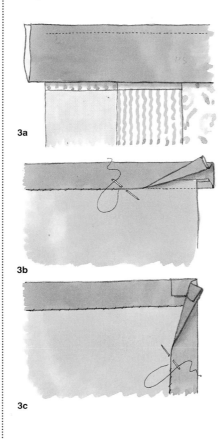

3a

3b

3c

The binding can also be added in a continuous strip as described for "Rail Fence" on page 84.

LABELLING

Always sign and date your quilt. If it's a present or for a special occasion you can add an inscription or message.

The simplest and most durable method is to embroider the words directly onto the back of the quilt.

To make a separate label, stitch the words onto a piece of plain muslin, or write with a permanent Pigma pen. Turn in the edges of the fabric and slip-stitch neatly to the back of the quilt.

DISPLAYING

If your quilt is to be displayed as a wallhanging or at a show it must have a sleeve attached on the reverse near the top through which a batten can be passed. A quilt should never be hung simply by pinning or by nails, which might damage it. It should be supported along its entire width to prevent stretching and distortion.

Adding a 3in/7.5cm Sleeve

1 Measure the width of the quilt and cut a 6½in/16.5cm strip to that measurement.

2 Fold it in half with right sides together. Sew the two ends together and along the open side, leaving a gap to turn the strip through (diagram 1).

3 Turn the strip right side out and close the gap with neat slipstitches.

4 Press well and attach to the back of the quilt at the top by slipstitching, making sure that the stitches don't show on the front (diagram 2).

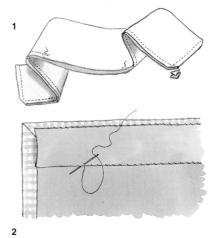

1

2

Sampler Patchwork Quilt

AN EXCELLENT INTRODUCTION TO PATCHWORK, A SAMPLER QUILT PROVIDES AN OPPORTUNITY TO WORK A SELECTION OF DIFFERENT BLOCK PATTERNS IN A VARIETY OF TECHNIQUES. THE BLOCKS IN THIS SMALL SAMPLER INCLUDE SIMPLE MACHINE AND HAND SEWN PIECING AND APPLIQUÉ, AS WELL AS GUIDELINES ON COLOUR, BUT TRY YOUR OWN COLOR SCHEME FOR AN INDIVIDUAL TOUCH. I HAVE USED NINE TRADITIONAL BLOCKS FOR THE CENTER OF THIS WALLHANGING, WITH FOUR LITTLE "OHIO STAR" BLOCKS TWINKLING IN THE CORNERS.

Size of quilt: 52 x 52in/132 x 132cm
Block sizes: 12in/30.5cm and 6in/15cm

MATERIALS

All fabrics used in quilt top and backing are 45in/115cm wide

- ▣ Template cardboard or plastic
- ▣ Borders and Sashing: 1½yards/1m 40cm dark blue fabric
- ▣ Binding: ½yard/45cm navy blue
- ▣ Backing: 2¾yards/2.7m

- ▣ Blocks: ½yard/45cm each of 6 different blue fabrics; ½yard/45cm each of 4 different cream fabrics; ½yard/45cm yellow fabric
- ▣ Batting: 2oz, 54 x 54in/136 x 136cm
- ▣ Quilting thread: dark blue

GENERAL CUTTING INSTRUCTIONS

1 Trace the templates given on pages 31 to 35 onto template cardboard or plastic and cut out accurately with sharp scissors. Label all the templates with the block name and letter and put in separate envelopes for each block.

2 Following the individual block instructions for the number of templates to cut and the fabric colour, place each template face down on the wrong side of the appropriate fabric and draw around the edges with a sharp pencil. (An "R" on a template indicates "reverse" and should be used face up on the reverse of the fabric.) Cut out on the drawn line. Note that except where indicated, the templates include a ¼in/0.75cm seam allowance.

3 For borders, cut four strips, 6½ x 40½in/16.5cm x 106.5cm, from blue fabric.

4 For sashings, cut twelve strips, 2½ x 12½in/7cm x 31.5cm, from blue fabric.

5 For sashing posts, cut four 2½in/7cm squares from yellow fabric.

6 Cut the binding fabric into strips 2½in/7cm wide.

7 Cut the backing fabric in half and stitch together to form a square 54 x 54in/136 x 136cm, cutting off the excess.

GENERAL STITCHING INSTRUCTIONS

Machine stitch using a 2.5 stitch length and taking an exact ¼in/0.75cm seam allowance. Press seam allowances to the darkest fabric. Piecing assembly diagrams and instructions are given with each block.

LOG CABIN

This is an alternative method to the foundation piecing used on page 120.

1 Cut a 2½in/6.5cm center square in blue, then the following strips in the colours indicated, changing the shade of the cream or blue every other strip, i.e. A and B cream are the same shade, B and C blue are the same (see diagram 4).
All the strips are 1¾in/4.5cm wide:
cream strip A, 2½in/6.5cm;
cream and blue strip B, 3¾in/9.5cm;
cream and blue strip C, 5in/12.5cm;
cream and blue strip D, 6¼in/15.5cm;
cream and blue strip E, 7½in/18.5cm;
cream and blue strip F, 8¾in/21.5cm;
cream and blue strip G, 10in/24.5cm;
cream and blue strip H, 11¼in/27.5cm;
blue strip I, 12½in/30.5cm;.

2 Begin with the center square and cream strip A. Place right sides together and stitch, taking a ¼in/0.75cm seam.

3 Open out, finger press, then add the cream strip B to the side of the first two pieces in the same way (diagram 1).

4 Add the blue strip B to the third side of the square and the side of the cream strip B (diagram 2).

5 Add the blue strip C to the final side of the square (diagram 3).

6 Continue working around the square in this way following the sequence in the diagram 4. Press all seams to one side away from the center.

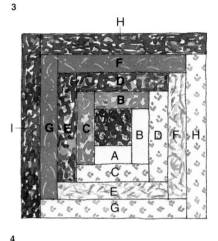

GOOSE TRACKS

Templates: A, B, C, D, E, F
This block introduces set-in piecing, where the seam between two patches is angled.

1 Cut the number of templates and in the colours as indicated on the templates (page 31).

2 Following the piecing diagram 5, stitch the four D diamonds together, then add piece C to the straight side of this group.

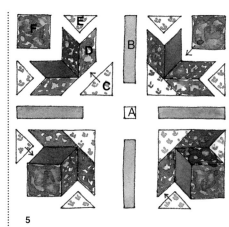

5

3 Next, set-in piece F. To do this, place F over D, right sides together, and start stitching at point a, stop at point b, lift the presser foot, pivot piece F until the adjacent side aligns with the second piece D, turn and stitch to point c (diagram 6). Press seams to one side.

4 Set-in piece E in the same way. Repeat to make three more groups, then add the sashing strips and posts as shown in diagram 7.

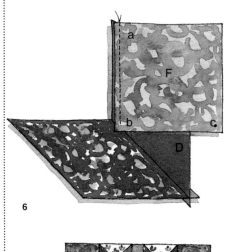

6

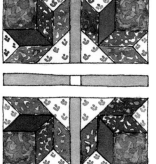

7

DRESDEN PLATE

Templates: A, B
This is my own method for creating points which is easier than using a pointed template and turning over the seam allowance.

1 Cut the number of templates and in the colours as indicated on the templates (page 31). Note when cutting the fabric from template B, you should add a ½in/1.5cm seam allowance. Cut one 12½in/31.5cm square from cream fabric for the background.

2 Fold one of the A pieces in half lengthways, right sides together, and sew a ¼in/0.75cm seam across the top (diagram 8).

3 Trim the seam and turn right side out, flatten and press to form a point (diagram 9).

4 Place two A pieces right sides together and, taking an exact ¼in/0.75cm seam allowance, machine stitch together (diagram 10). Continue

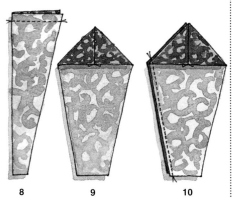

8   **9**   **10**

joining the other A pieces until you have a complete circle of sixteen. Press all seams to one side.

5 Fold the cream background square in half lengthwise and crosswise and finger press the folds to find the center. Appliqué the pieced circle in the center, using blue thread to match the "plate". Take small stitches and tuck the needle slightly under the appliqué to hide the stitch (see page 51).

6 Make a running stitch around the outside of the center circle B, place the template on the wrong side of the circle and draw up the gathering tightly, pulling the fabric around the template, and press. Gently remove the template and you have a perfect circle.

7 Appliqué this to the center of the "plate" to complete the block.

3D MAPLE

Templates: A, AR, B, C, D, DR
This block requires accurate piecing to ensure that all points meet neatly in the center.

1 Cut the number of templates and in the colors as indicated on the templates (page 32).

2 Follow the piecing diagrams 11 and 12, setting-in the pieced corner squares as described for the "Goose Tracks" block above.

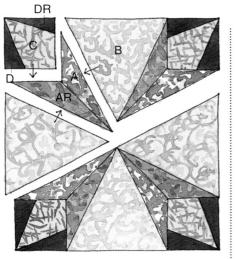

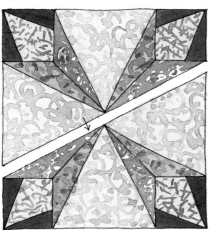

11

12

MARINER'S COMPASS

Templates: A, B, C, D, E, F
This block is often regarded as one of
the most complex to piece, but accurate
cutting and sewing will ensure that the
block lays flat and the points are sharp.

1   Cut the number of templates and
in the colors as indicated on the
templates (page 33).

2   Follow the piecing diagrams 13
to 16 to stitch the "compass".

3   Sew the four piece Es together to
form the background square. Clip all
the curved edges (diagram 17).

4   Pin around the pieced circle,
right sides together, matching the points
of D to the seams of E and stitch.

5   Make and appliqué the center
circle as for "Dresden Plate" above.

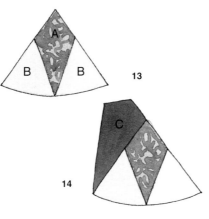

13

14

15

16

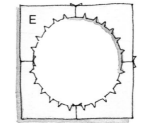

17

PUSS IN THE CORNER

Templates: A, B, C, D, E
This block, which introduces a large
number of elements to piece, is based
on a nine patch square.

1   Cut the number of templates and
in the colors as indicated on the
templates (page 34).

2   Following the piecing diagrams
18 and 19, join the pieces into squares
first, then the squares into rows and
finally join the rows together.

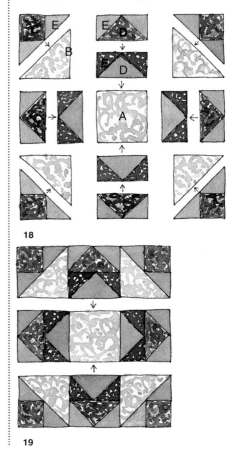

18

19

CLAMSHELLS

Template A

This is a hand-sewn traditional English patchwork block.

1   Cut one background 12½in/31.5cm square from cream fabric.

2   Fold in half horizontally, then vertically, and finger press the folds lightly to find the center.

3   Draw around Template A (page 32) on the wrong side of the appropriate fabric and cut out adding a ¼in/0.75cm seam allowance. Cut a total of twenty from assorted blue and cream fabrics.

4   Run a gathering stitch around the curve just inside the raw edge. Place Template A back on the drawn pencil marking on the wrong side (diagram 20) and, holding fabric and template firmly, pull up the gathering to fit snugly around the template edge.

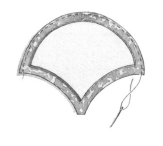

20

5   Holding the template in place, press and remove template. Repeat for all the clamshells.

6   Pin the first row of four clamshells, aligning the side points with the bottom raw edge of the background square keeping within the seam allowance at the sides of the square. The bottom points of these four clamshells will overhang the edge – these can be trimmed off when the block is completed (diagram 21).

21

7   Tuck the next row of three clamshells behind the first four, making sure all raw edges are hidden behind the first row (diagram 22).

22

8   Add the next row of two clamshells and finally the last one, with the top clamshell in the center. Repeat for the opposite side of the square.

9   Appliqué all the clamshells in place, using a matching thread.

STORM AT SEA

Templates: A, B, C, D, E, F, FR, G

This block, when set together in a quilt, gives the impression of curves when in fact all the edges are straight. Even in just one block the effect is apparent.

1   Cut the number of templates and in the colors as indicated on the templates (page 35).

2   Follow the piecing diagrams 23 and 24 to stitch the block.

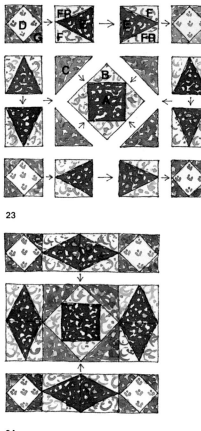

23

24

CARD TRICK
Templates A, B
Be sure to follow the coloring plan to achieve the 3D look of this block.

1   Cut the number of templates and in the colors as indicated on the templates (page 34).

2   Following the piecing diagrams 25 and 26, join the triangles into squares first, then the squares into rows and finally join the rows together.

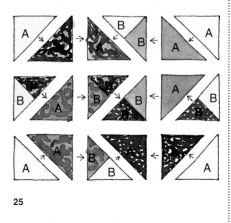

25

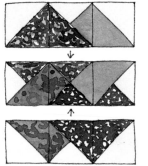

26

OHIO STAR (Corner Blocks)
Templates: A, B
A simple nine patch block which can be used on its own to make a very effective quilt.

1   Cut the number of templates and in the colours as indicated on the templates (page 32).

2   Follow the piecing diagrams 27 and 28. Make four blocks.

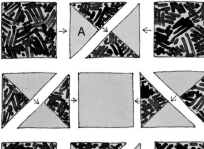

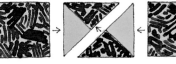

27

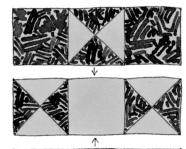

28

ASSEMBLING
1   Trim all nine blocks for the center of the quilt to measure 12½in/31.5cm square and trim the corner blocks to measure 6½in/16.5cm square, taking care not to cut into the block design.

2   Lay the center blocks out following the quilt assembly plan (page 24) and number them 1 to 9, pinning the numbers in the top left-hand corner.

3   Following the quilt assembly plan, sew two sashing strips between blocks 1, 2 and 3.

Take a sashing strip and sew a post to the short right-hand end, then add a second sashing strip, second post and third sashing strip to complete the sashing row.

Sew this along the bottom edge of the top row, being careful to match all the seams.

Continue in this way, making rows of blocks, then rows of sashing and posts, until the top is complete.

ADDING BORDERS
1   Determine the length of the borders by measuring the quilt top from center top edge to center bottom edge. Trim the four cut strips to this measurement.

2   Stitch two of the border strips to the top and bottom of the quilt. Press the seams towards the borders.

3   Sew one corner block to each end of the remaining two borders, then stitch these borders to the quilt sides, again making sure all seams match.

FINISHING
1   Layer the backing, batting and quilt top taking care to smooth out any wrinkles (see page 37).

2   Run rows of basting, about 4in/10cm apart from top to bottom and side to side across the quilt.

3   I have quilted this quilt by hand using a variety of patterns for each block and using a contrast dark blue quilting thread, but it could easily be quilted on the machine using a "stipple" pattern (see page 37) on all the cream pieces.

4   Join the binding strips together to the required length and bind the quilt with a double-fold binding.

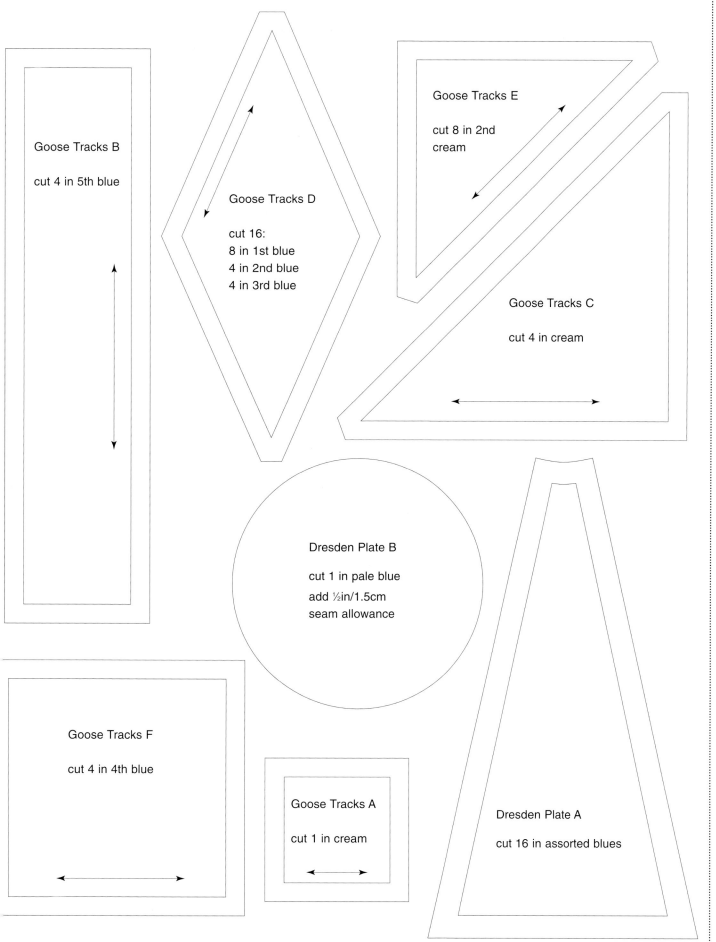

Goose Tracks B

cut 4 in 5th blue

Goose Tracks D

cut 16:
8 in 1st blue
4 in 2nd blue
4 in 3rd blue

Goose Tracks E

cut 8 in 2nd
cream

Goose Tracks C

cut 4 in cream

Dresden Plate B

cut 1 in pale blue
add ½in/1.5cm
seam allowance

Goose Tracks F

cut 4 in 4th blue

Goose Tracks A

cut 1 in cream

Dresden Plate A

cut 16 in assorted blues

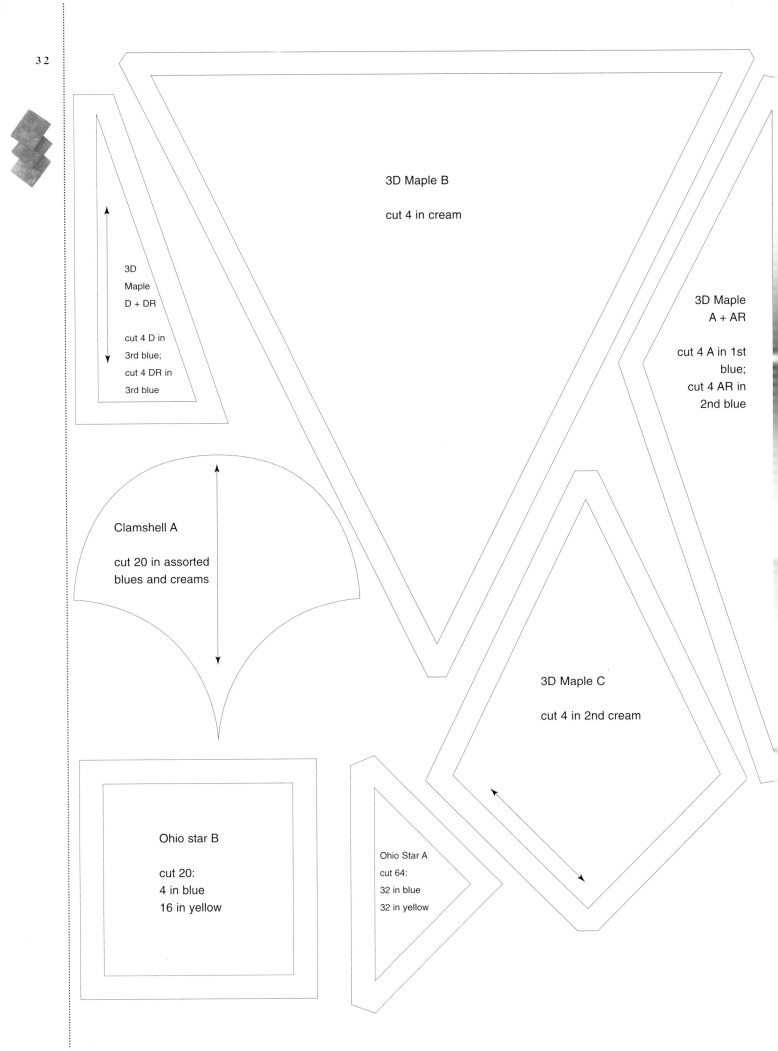

3D Maple B

cut 4 in cream

3D
Maple
D + DR

cut 4 D in
3rd blue;
cut 4 DR in
3rd blue

3D Maple
A + AR

cut 4 A in 1st
blue;
cut 4 AR in
2nd blue

Clamshell A

cut 20 in assorted
blues and creams

3D Maple C

cut 4 in 2nd cream

Ohio star B

cut 20:
4 in blue
16 in yellow

Ohio Star A
cut 64:
32 in blue
32 in yellow

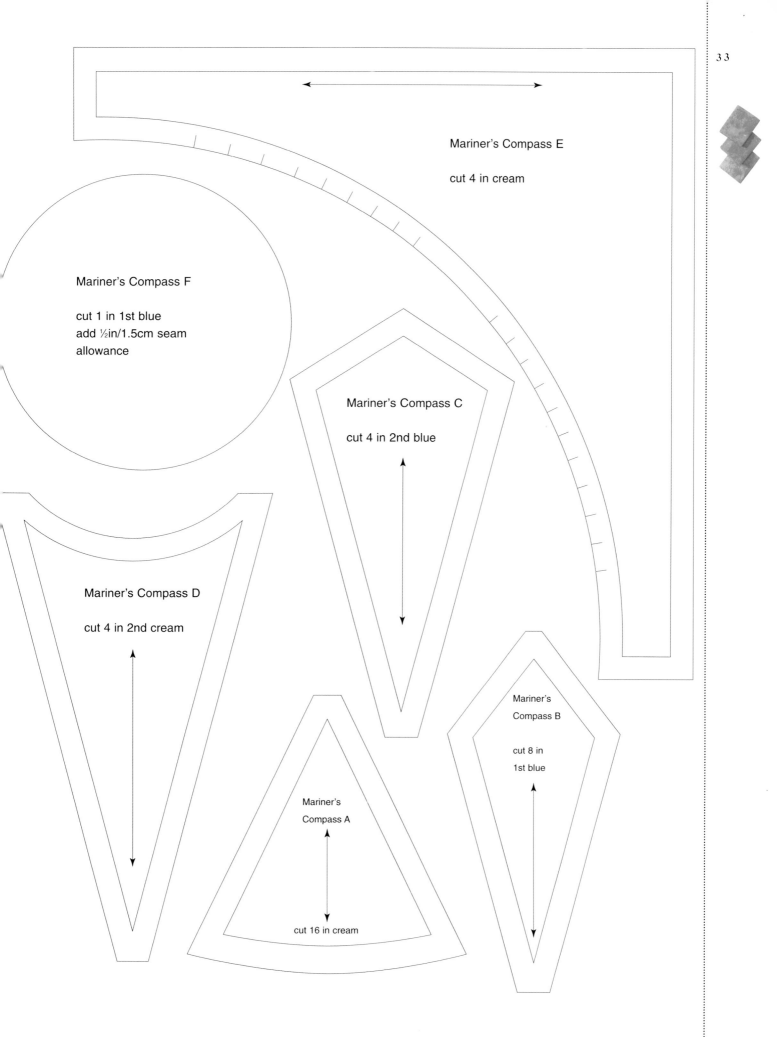

Mariner's Compass E

cut 4 in cream

Mariner's Compass F

cut 1 in 1st blue
add ½in/1.5cm seam
allowance

Mariner's Compass C

cut 4 in 2nd blue

Mariner's Compass D

cut 4 in 2nd cream

Mariner's
Compass B

cut 8 in
1st blue

Mariner's
Compass A

cut 16 in cream

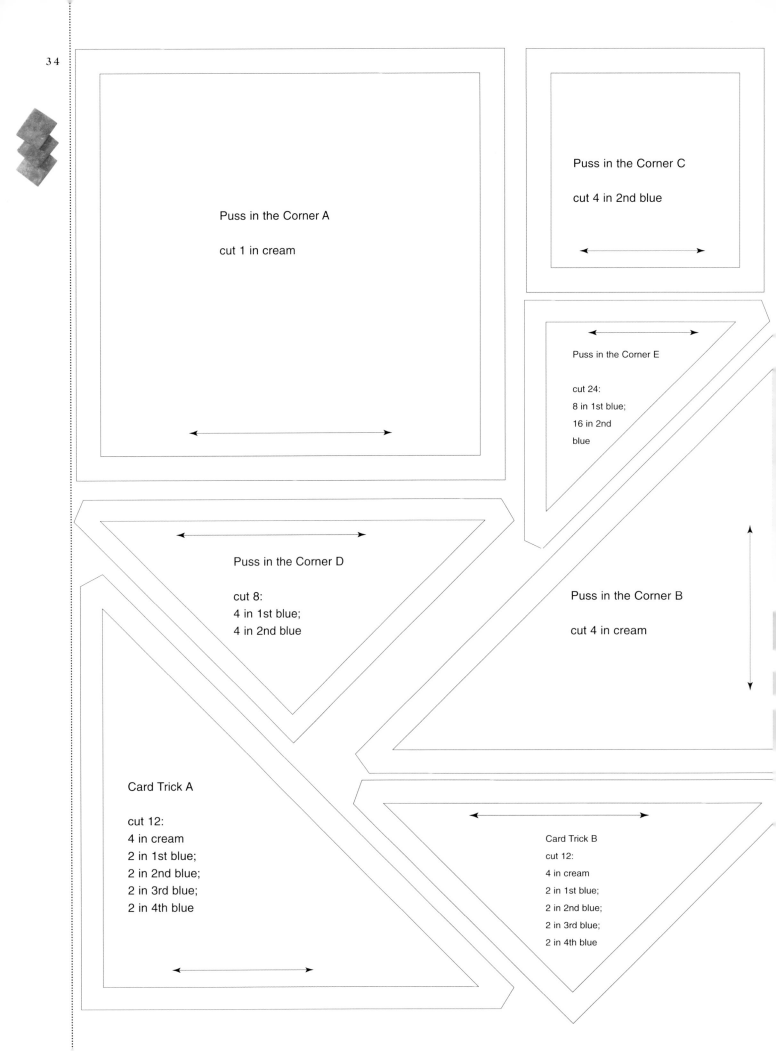

Puss in the Corner A

cut 1 in cream

Puss in the Corner C

cut 4 in 2nd blue

Puss in the Corner E

cut 24:
8 in 1st blue;
16 in 2nd
blue

Puss in the Corner D

cut 8:
4 in 1st blue;
4 in 2nd blue

Puss in the Corner B

cut 4 in cream

Card Trick A

cut 12:
4 in cream
2 in 1st blue;
2 in 2nd blue;
2 in 3rd blue;
2 in 4th blue

Card Trick B

cut 12:
4 in cream
2 in 1st blue;
2 in 2nd blue;
2 in 3rd blue;
2 in 4th blue

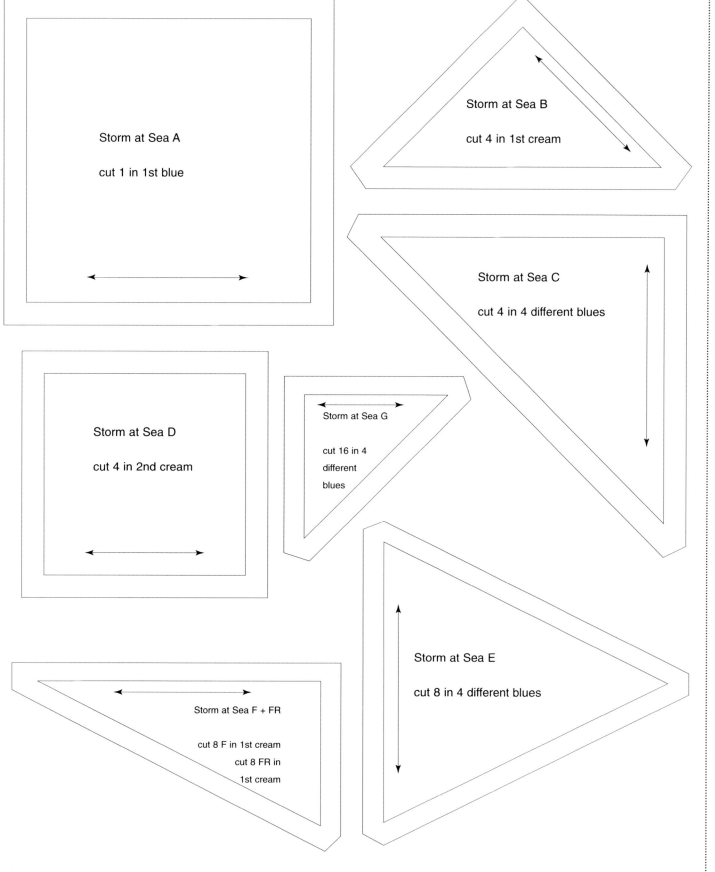

Storm at Sea A

cut 1 in 1st blue

Storm at Sea B

cut 4 in 1st cream

Storm at Sea C

cut 4 in 4 different blues

Storm at Sea D

cut 4 in 2nd cream

Storm at Sea G

cut 16 in 4
different
blues

Storm at Sea E

cut 8 in 4 different blues

Storm at Sea F + FR

cut 8 F in 1st cream
cut 8 FR in
1st cream

QUILTING

Quilting is a versatile craft, which can be purely functional, purely decorative, or both at once. At its simplest, it's a way of anchoring layers of fabric together so that they form a single textile. This is usually achieved by the use of a running stitch, which passes through all the layers. At its most sophisticated, it can transform a craft into a fine art. So, when you're thinking about which style and method to use for a particular project, it makes sense to consider both practical purpose and decorative effect.

The practical considerations concern how dense the quilt stitching needs to be in order to prevent the batting from bunching up (see page 22). Possibilities for decorative quilting include whether you want the stitching to be in a contrast color to emphasize the pattern, whether you will use the quilting design to disguise pieced seams, and whether you wish to add motifs to reflect the theme of the quilt.

A further initial decision is whether to quilt by hand or machine. Machine-quilting is quicker but does need some practice in manipulating a large area of layered fabric in the sewing machine.

Quilting designs consist of motifs, border patterns and infill designs. A selection of designs for each type is given on pages 42 and 43. On a whole-cloth quilt all three would be used.

MARKING DESIGNS

The quilting pattern can either be marked out on the quilt surface before it's layered or, if the pattern is suitable (e.g. a simple repeat pattern), it can be marked one section at a time while the quilt is in the frame or hoop.

Using Stencils

There are many commercially produced stencils to choose from or you can make your own from cardboard or

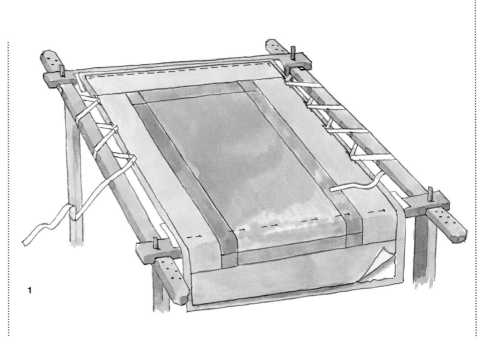

1

template plastic, either freehand or by drawing around household objects, such as wine glasses and plates, to make up your designs. Draw around the stencils with a #2 pencil, chinagraph pencil or other marker (see page 9).

Tracing

1   Trace the pattern onto tracing paper, using a felt pen or dark crayon. Lay the pattern under the quilt surface.

2   Mark the quilt top with a pencil or other marker, moving the tracing around as needed if the pattern is to be repeated. If the quilt top is of light colored fabric, the pattern will show through clearly enough to be followed. To mark onto darker fabrics, use a light-box if available, or use sticky tape to fix the pattern and the quilt to a window.

Dressmakers' Carbon Paper

This is an easy and efficient way to transfer patterns to quilt tops and is a good way to mark dark fabrics.

1   Lay the carbon paper face down on the quilt and the pattern on top.

2   Trace over the pattern, using firm pressure.

Masking Tape

Geometric designs can be marked with ruled lines or by sticking on strips of masking tape.

WORKING IN A FRAME

The great advantage of using a frame is that the quilt sandwich doesn't need to be basted in a grid.

1   Use basting stitches to attach the backing fabric to the webbing on one of the rails and stretch it over to the opposite rail. Pin to the webbing, stretching gently to ensure that it's smooth. Leave the excess to hang over the rail.

2   Lay the batting and the quilt top over the backing and baste these also to the rail. Stretch them over to the opposite rail and pin over the backing.

3   Adjust the tension by pinning tapes onto the sides of the quilt and attaching them to the stretchers, i.e. the side rails (diagram 1).

4 When quilting of the first section is completed, remove the pins and wind that section around the top rail until the next part is exposed. Pin again and continue quilting.

WORKING IN A HOOP OR BY MACHINE

For both these methods it's necessary to firmly baste the entire quilt surface so that the three layers don't move while you're quilting. Although this is quite a long task, it's time well spent because it will make the quilting quicker, easier and of better quality. The following instructions are for basting by the traditional method although some short cuts include holding the layers together with safety pins, plastic tacks and spray-on glue.

1 Work on a table or other large work space. As a last resort, work on the floor, although this is quite hard on the knees and back.

2 Lay out first the backing, wrong side up, then the batting and finally the quilt top, right side up. Center the quilt top over the other layers, leaving an extra 2in/5cm of batting and backing all around.

3 Stretch and smooth the whole sandwich as evenly as possible, then pin at regular intervals using long, glass-headed pins.

Tip *To keep the quilt stretched and under tension while pinning and basting, try weighting it on all sides, for example with books. Another tip is to clamp the quilt to the sides of a table using large bulldog clips.*

4 Using a large needle, baste evenly over the quilt surface with 2in/5cm stitches. Start from the center and either work diagonally into the corners or in straight rows towards either end (diagram 2). Rows of stitches should be placed at intervals of about 4in/10cm. Remove pins as you go.

QUILTING BY HAND

Whether you're quilting in a hoop or on a frame, the section you're working on must be kept under tension, so that the layers don't move apart. Make sure that the backing (under the hoop or frame) and the top are both completely smooth. Tension should be set just firmly enough to enable you to push the needle easily up and down through all layers.

To start quilting, wear a thimble on the second finger of your right hand, preferably one with a raised rim and, if preferred, a finger guard on the index finger of your left hand. Work with the right hand on top of the quilt and the left underneath.

1 Work with pieces of quilting thread no longer than 18in/46cm . Thread into a betweens needle and make a knot in the end. Bring the thread up from the back through all the layers of material and gently pull the knot through the backing into the batting. Take a small backstitch, bringing the needle back on top.

2 Insert the needle through all the layers. The needle should be inserted straight into the fabric, not at an angle.

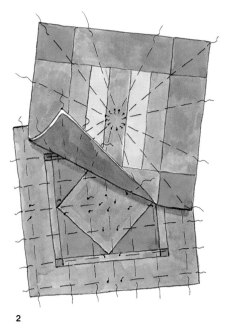

2

Lodging the needle against the rim of the thimble makes it easy to pass the needle through the layers by an unforced rocking movement. On the underside of the quilt, position your left hand so that the finger underneath the needle can gently push up the section of fabric just in front of the needle. You should be able to feel the point of the needle at each stitch.

3 Push the needle back up through the surface a short distance from where it was inserted and just far enough through the fabric sandwich to be able to take another small stitch. The actual size of the quilting stitch isn't important unless you particularly want to aim at very fine quilting. What is important is that the stitches and the gaps between them should be of even size and that the stitches should go through all the layers.

3

4 Work in this way, developing a rocking movement with the needle, until you have three or four stitches on the needle (diagram 3), then pull it completely through the surface of the quilt and draw up the thread to give firm but not taut stitches.

5 At the end of the piece of thread, make a knot in the thread close to the surface of the quilt, then make a small back stitch, inserting the needle into the batting and bringing it back up onto the surface a short distance away. Pull on the thread until the knot pops beneath the surface and there is no surplus thread. Cut off the thread.

QUICK OR UTILITY QUILTING METHODS

Hand-quilting was raised to a fine art by some exceptional women – particularly American women – for whom it was both an ideal relaxation and a medium for personal creative expression. Traditionally for most people, though, quilting was for use, not show. What was important was to get the job done quickly, efficiently and cheaply. Two of the most common ways of doing this were by quilting with big stitches and by tying.

Quilting with Big Stitches

If you look at old quilts you'll see that many of them have been simply and efficiently quilted with big stitches. Provided that the stitches are of even size, this method gives quick and pleasing results. Use a needle with a large eye, such as a crewel needle, and soft, thick thread such as pearl cotton. The quilting method is the same as for any other hand-quilting but you take bigger stitches onto the needle. Use a contrasting color for maximum decorative effect.

Tying

Tying is a quick and effective way to finish a quilt. In America quilts finished this way are often called "comforters" because they are light and soft but warm. The batting does not become so compressed as when it's quilted, giving it a higher loft.

1 Use soft, strong thread, such as pearl cotton or double knitting wool, and a large needle. If you want the ties to show as a decorative feature, choose a color to contrast with the quilt top. Ties should be placed at regular intervals, say 4 to 6in/10 to 15cm apart, or at chosen points in the pattern in the case of a patchwork top.

2 Insert the needle from the top through all layers, leaving a tail of about 4in/10cm. Bring the needle back up a short distance from where it entered, then take another stitch through the same holes. Cut off the thread, leaving another 4in/10cm tail and tie the tails together with a double knot (diagram 4).

3 Trim the ends to leave about 1in/3cm of the threads showing.

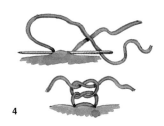

4

"Quilt As You Go"

Assembling and quilting a large quilt can seem a daunting task. An alternative is the "quilt as you go" method, in which each block is quilted separately so that you are only dealing with small units. Blocks are layered with batting and lining and quilted one at a time and are only joined when they are all completed.

1 After each block is pieced, cut a piece of batting and a piece of lining, allowing at least an 1½in/4cm extra all around the block. Layer and baste the block and place it in a hoop. Tack a temporary border around the block (diagram 5).

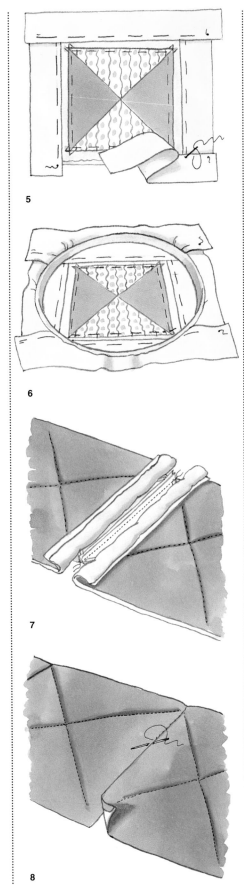

5

6

7

8

2   Place the block in a hoop, adjusting tension so that you can easily move the needle through the layers. Quilt the block but do not quilt over the seam allowances or you won't be able to join the blocks (diagram 6).

3   When all the blocks have been quilted, lay them out in the correct order for assembly. First join them in rows. Pin back the batting and backing fabric and join the pieced tops, right sides together (diagram 7).

4   Working from the back of the quilt, trim the batting between the blocks, so that the edges meet but do not overlap. Stitch together using ladder-stitch or herringbone stitch.

5   Join the backing fabric by smoothing it down on one unit, leaving the edge rough. Fold under the edge of the next unit and neatly hem it over the rough edge (diagram 8).

6   When all the blocks have been joined in rows, join the rows together. To do this, repeat steps three, four and five above for joining the pieced blocks, then the batting and, finally, the backing.

QUILTING BY MACHINE

There are two methods, one for patterns which can be stitched in straight lines, the other for "free" designs. For either method, make sure you have plenty of table space beside and behind the machine to support the quilt while you're working.

Tip   *It's worth spending time making some samplers and practising quilting on them before you graduate to a full-size quilt.*

Method 1

If you're just learning to machine-quilt, it's advisable to start with straight line quilting. Outline quilting, patterns like diamonds and quilting "in-the-ditch"

(see below) are sensible designs with which to begin.

1   Attach a walking foot. Adjust the tension on your machine to be a little looser than for normal sewing.

2   Roll the quilt from one edge, leaving just enough of it free to work on (diagram 9).

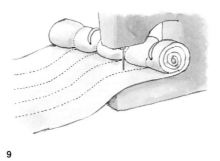

9

Tip   *The rolled part of the quilt can be secured with bicycle clips.*

3   As you stitch, use both hands to hold the quilt firmly on either side of the needle (diagram 10). Start and finish with a few reversed stitches and once the stitching is complete, thread the ends into a needle and draw them in between the fabric layers for a short distance, bring the needle to the surface again and tie off.

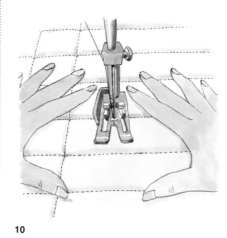

10

Method 2

For free-motion machine quilting, you need to be able to adjust your machine

for flatbed sewing. The footplate must be flush with the table top, so that you can move the quilt around smoothly. If your machine does not have a special table with a well for the machine to drop into, you will need to make or buy an extension to fit the machine.

1   Attach a darning foot, adjust the stitch length to 0 and slightly lower the needle tension.

2   Place the section of the quilt to be worked on in a traditional quilting hoop. Alternatively, use a special plastic half-hoop, which grips and holds the quilt while you work.

3   Run the machine at a slightly slower rate than for normal sewing. Lower the presser foot and start the machine. Hold the hoop firmly between both hands and guide the needle along the quilting lines (diagram 11).

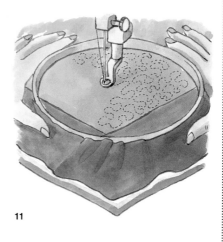

11

Tip   *The secret of successful free-motion machine quilting is to keep the hoop moving under the needle at a steady rate. If you move it too slowly, the stitches will be too tiny. If you move it too fast, the stitches will be too large.*

4   To finish the quilting, take a few stitches with the needle stationary and snip off threads.

TYPES OF QUILTING

QUILTING "IN THE DITCH"

This method is suitable for pieced patchwork. Quilting stitches are worked exactly on top of the joining seams so that they are invisible. This is ideal if the purpose of the quilting is simply to anchor the layers together. It's a very quick and easy method and can be done by hand or machine.

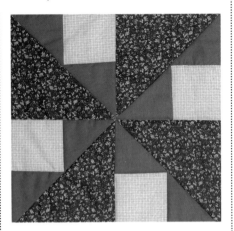

OUTLINE QUILTING

Another method of quilting pieced patchwork is to quilt around the patches, usually about ¼in/0.75cm away from the seam. The quilting lines can be marked using a ruler. With a little practice, though, most quilters learn to trust their eye, so avoiding the need for marking. It can be done by hand or machine. This is another straightforward method, which accentuates the piecing design.

WHOLECLOTH QUILTING

In contrast to patchwork, or pieced tops, the decorative effect of a whole-cloth quilt comes entirely from the quilting pattern which is worked by hand on an unpieced fabric. "Strippy quilts" are a variation on wholecloth quilts. They are made up of broad strips of cloth and have the patterns marked within the strips. Stencils or traced drawings are used for marking both wholecloth and strippy quilts.

ECHO QUILTING

In echo quilting, also called Hawaiian quilting, the line of hand or machine-

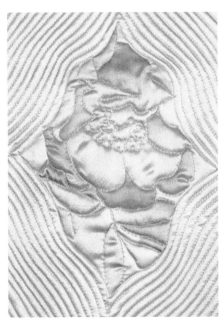

quilting stitches follows the outline of shapes on the quilt top. Several rows of quilting are used around each shape and the shapes themselves are often appliquéd.

RANDOM QUILTING

Also called meander or vermicelli quilting, this is an infill pattern worked by free-motion machine quilting, the result resembling squiggles.

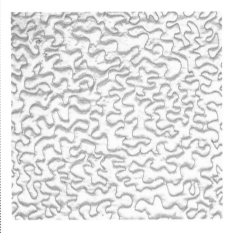

FLAT QUILTING

Flat quilting simply means that two layers of fabric are joined by quilting stitches. This is a technique often used to make such items as light summer coverlets. Varieties of flat quilting include two Italian forms of quilting: trapunto and corded quilting. Corded quilting is often referred to as Italian quilting. Shadow quilting is in effect a variation of corded quilting.

Trapunto

Trapunto is a way of adding texture to the surface of a quilt. Sections of the quilting motif, worked by hand or machine, are selected and small pieces of batting are pushed up into them from the back of the quilt through tiny slits made in the backing fabric. The slits are then neatly re-sewn. If the backing fabric is of sufficiently loose weave, holes for the stuffing can be made by separating the fibres and easing them back together when the stuffing is completed.

Corded or Italian Quilting

This is a highly decorative quilting technique much used on clothes and quilts in the 17th and 18th centuries. Double lines of stitching form a channel through which cord is passed, making a raised pattern. The channels can be stitched by hand or machine, the width of the channel depending on the thickness of the cord to be used.

Shadow Quilting

True shadow quilting is really a variation of corded quilting. The top layer of fabric is fine gauze. Cord of contrasting color to the background is threaded through the channels made by the lines of quilting. This produces a pattern in subtly muted colors.

Nowadays the phrase "shadow quilting" is often wrongly used to describe what is really shadow appliqué. In this technique, appliquéd shapes are covered with fine see-through fabric, then anchored by quilting around the shapes.

ETHNIC QUILTING

Many countries have developed their own characteristic styles and methods, some of which provide a rich source of inspiration for contemporary quiltmakers. In Britain, the influence of the traditional quilting patterns and styles of the North East of England and of Wales is still very much alive. Many other cultures have developed their own quilting styles and techniques. Two examples are the sashiko technique from Japan and the techniques used in the kanthas of Northern India.

Sashiko

Sashiko means "little stabs" and is a form of decorative hand stitching which is a cross between quilting and embroidery. It was originally used by country people to make warm clothing as protection against the bitter Japanese winters. As women gained more leisure time, and ready-made cotton clothing became more easily available, the sashiko technique was elaborated into the decorative style of today. The use of white stitching on indigo-dyed fabric is characteristic of the modern style.

Kanthas

Kanthas are part of the folk tradition of Bangladesh. They are quilts built up of layers of worn cloth (these often include old saris), which are stitched together and embellished with embroidery in the form of densely worked running stitches. The embroidery frequently involves pictures of people and animals and symbols with religious significance, such as the Tree of Life. The quilter also often depicts common objects from her own life, for example, kitchen utensils, jewellery or toilet articles. Kanthas are given as gifts and used as swaddling clothes for babies.

QUILTING MOTIFS

infill design

Amish Aspirations border

patch motifs

Amish Aspirations center

narrow border or infill design

ENGLISH PIECING

Making patchwork by basting patches of fabric over paper templates before oversewing them together by hand has become universally known as "English Piecing", to distinguish it from the American method in which the fabric patches are simply sewn right sides together by hand or machine with a running stitch.

Most early examples of patchwork using English piecing are coverlets rather than quilts. That is, they weren't padded but were finished simply with a lining. Paper templates, which are sometimes found still stitched into position in antique quilts, can give fascinating glimpses into the life and times of their makers, providing valuable information for social historians.

English piecing was mostly done by relatively affluent women, who had the time for such labour-intensive work. Its heyday was in the Victorian period, when it became the height of fashion as a pastime for such women. Among quiltmakers nowadays it has a rather poor reputation, perhaps because of its association with what we see as the restricted lives and values of the Victorian women who were so fond of it. As a result, it's often dismissed as an unnecessarily fiddly and time-consuming technique, only suited for women who indeed had all too much time to consume, and not at all appropriate for the busy lives of contemporary quilters.

This is less than fair. Though no-one would claim that English piecing is a speedy technique, it is, in fact, one which can be both effective and versatile. It offers unique possibilities for design in the use of fabric, pattern and color as well as some useful practical advantages. There are surviving Victorian and earlier examples which clearly show the level of artistry which it is possible to attain through its use.

English piecing is also sometimes referred to as "Mosaic" piecing. This name usefully indicates the interesting geometrical effects which can be pro-duced more easily by this method than by any other. It is indeed a perfect method for accurately piecing intricate patterns, especially those involving shapes with awkward angles.

It's also a technique which is custom-made for those who still cherish the notion of patchwork as a creative way of using up leftover scraps of fabric. One of the great exponents of this method was the children's writer, Lucy Boston, who vividly describes the sheer joy of rummaging through a scrap bag to find exactly the right color and texture of fabric to place in a pattern.

FABRICS

Cottons, silks and other lightweight fabrics can all be used. The English piecing method is also particularly suitable in patchworks where you want to use a variety of fabrics of different weights and textures. This becomes much easier once the fabrics have been basted to papers.

METHOD

A template made of metal or thick cardboard is needed for each shape you want to use. You can also use template plastic provided it's the thick, rigid sort. You also need a paper template for each fabric patch. Heavy quality paper is best but it shouldn't be so thick that it's difficult to pierce with your needle. This is where "junk mail" can be put to good use, as such leaflets and brochures often use paper of just the right quality. So, not only are you recycling fabric, you're also recycling paper!

1   Use the metal or cardboard template to draw the shape on paper and cut it out. You can manage this stage of the process more quickly and accurately by cutting several paper templates at the same time. Place the master template

over two or three layers of paper, hold them firmly with your left hand and cut, running the blade of the scissors closely along the edge of the template.

2   Next use the paper template to cut the fabric patches. Pin one of the paper shapes onto the chosen fabric and cut around it, leaving a generous seam allowance, about ⅜in/1cm (diagram 1).

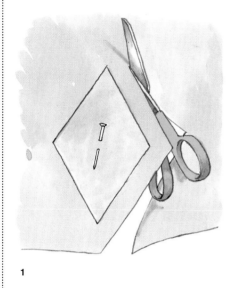

1

3   Turn the seam allowance over the edge of the paper and baste it down all around. Turn in the corners and baste (diagrams 2 to 5).

4   To sew the patches together, make a knot in the thread. Place two patches right sides together and bring the thread through from the back of one of them so that the knot is concealed in the seam (diagram 6).

5   Oversew the two edges together with small stitches. Work from corner to corner, trying to run the stitches as straight as possible across the two edges. At the end of the seam, take a few backstitches, then snip the thread (diagram 7).

6   When a third patch is to be added into a tight angle, it's tempting

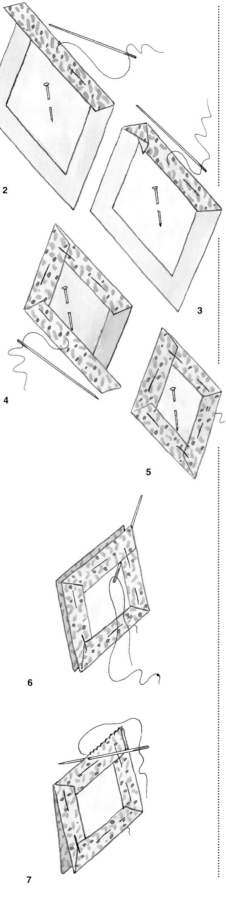

2

3

4

5

6

7

simply to re-align the patches and sew the next seam with one continuous thread. You'll get a stronger join, however, if you secure the end of each seam as described above before adding the new patch.

7   If you like your patchwork to look as neat at the back as it does on the front, you can use a window template. This is the same shape as a solid template but it is ¼in/0.75cm larger all around with the center cut out. Using it allows you to mark both the sewing line and the seam allowance, which will then be exactly the same all around the patch. You can also use it to select particular areas of a patterned fabric to appear on each fabric patch. Move the template over the right side of the fabric until you see the required portion in the template window, then mark (diagram 8).

8

Tumbling Blocks Crib Quilt

In America, optical illusion patterns are vividly described as "eye-foolers". "Tumbling Blocks" is one of the easiest of them to make. Only one template is needed, a 60° diamond. The three-dimensional illusion is achieved by using dark, medium and light fabrics. In this quilt we've used only three fabrics but this pattern is also very effective made up as a scrap quilt. The cover is finished by the tying method. The edges are bound.

Quilt size: 26 x 30in/66 x 77cm

Materials

- Template plastic or thick cardboard for the diamond template
- Firm paper for the paper templates
- Fabrics: ¼yd/23cm each of three fabrics: dark, medium and light
- Threads to match your fabrics, or one neutral color
- Backing: ⅞yd/70cm in a coordinating color
- Borders: an extra ¼yard/23cm – either repeat a fabric

from those chosen or select a different one to tone with them
- Size 8 pearl cotton in a coordinating color. (This is for tying the quilt. You can also use several strands of embroidery silks or hand-quilting thread for the tying. Use a contrasting color if you want the ends of the ties to show.)
- Batting: 2oz, 28 x 32in/79 x 68cm
- Binding: ⅓yard/12in of matching or contrasting fabric

CUTTING

1 Trace the template on page 49 onto cardboard or template plastic and cut out.

2 Use the template to cut 114 paper patterns.

3 Pin the paper patterns to the wrong side of the fabric and cut around each one, leaving about $\frac{3}{8}$in/1cm seam allowance all the way around. Cut:
35 patches of dark material;
35 patches of medium material;
44 patches of light material.

STITCHING

Follow diagrams 2 to 5 in the general instructions given for English Piecing (pages 44 to 45).

1 Lay out a row of dark and medium patches as shown (diagram 1).

2 Join the patches in a row, then add a row of light patches. Add a second row of light and dark patches (diagram 2).

3 Continue in this way, until all rows of diamond patches have been stitched together, beginning and ending with a light row (diagram 3).

4 When the patchwork is complete, gently press the top with the papers still in place. There will be extra half diamonds at the edges of the finished patchwork but leave these until you add the borders.

5 Remove the basting stitches from the patches and pull out the papers. Leave the turnings on the patches around the outside folded under.

Tip *If you're careful in removing the papers you can re-use them in another project.*

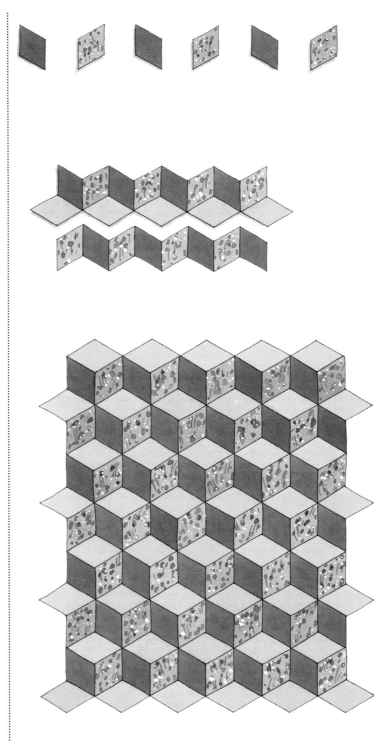

1

2

3

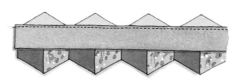

4

ADDING BORDERS

1   Determine the length of the top and bottom borders by measuring the quilt top from edge to edge across the center. Cut two 4in/10cm wide strips of that length from medium fabric (or contrasting fabric if preferred).

2   With right sides together, pin strips to the top and bottom of the cover, leaving the half diamonds showing at the edges (diagram 4).

3   Stitch the strips to the cover. Take a ¼in/0.75cm seam allowance on the border strip but stitch as closely as possible to the junctions of the patches.

4   Determine the length of the side borders by measuring the quilt top from edge to edge through the center, including the newly-added borders. Cut two 4in/10cm strips to this measurement and add to the sides of the cover, stitching as closely as possible to the edges of the patches.

5   Cut off the extra half diamonds and press the border flat.

6   When the cover is complete, gently press with a cool iron, taking care not to stretch the patchwork.

FINISHING

1   Cut a 28 x 32in/68 x 79in piece for the backing. Press well and lay it out, wrong side up.

2   Place the batting over it and position the top of the quilt, right side up, so that it is centered on the batting. Pin through all three layers.

3   Baste the layers together.

4   Following the basic instructions for tying a quilt (page 38), make a tie in the corner of each diamond patch using pearl cotton, embroidery or quilting thread.

5   Trim the backing and batting even with the top.

6   Cut 3in/8cm wide strips to fit the top and bottom of the cover. Fold the strips in half wrong sides together and press well.

7   Pin the strips to the right side of the top and bottom of the quilt, aligning the raw edges, and stitch, taking a ½in/1.5cm seam allowance.

8   Press the binding to the back of the quilt and hem it to the backing.

9   Cut 3in/8cm wide strips to fit the sides of the cover, adding 1½in/4cm for turnings at each end. Add them to the sides of the quilt as before. Press binding to the back, turn in the raw edges at the corners and hem as before.

10   Finally, don't forget to add a label showing your name, the date and any message you want to include.

Tumbling Blocks
Template

APPLIQUÉ

Appliqué is the term used for stitching a contrasting piece or pieces of fabric to a background piece to make a pattern and is one of the earliest ways of decorating fabric. It is used in quiltmaking in many forms. One of its great advantages is that many different kinds of fabrics can be used.

Appliqué can be worked by hand or machine and the edges of the applied pieces can be dealt with in a variety of ways, depending on the intended use of the article and your own skills and preferences. Appliqué can also be combined with other quiltmaking techniques – for example to stitch English pieced rosettes of hexagons onto a larger piece of fabric.

For your quilt to hang well, it is important that the appliquéd piece and the background fabric remain equally flat as they are being worked. Embroiderers recommend working appliqué in a frame for this reason, or you can layer the fabrics on a flat sur-face and baste securely. One of the rules that I try not to break is about the grain of the fabric – try to have the straight of the grain for the background fabric and the appliqué motifs running the same way. This is something that you need to consider when you are making your templates (see below) and cutting out the fabric shapes.

For information on suitable fabrics, see page 67.

MAKING APPLIQUÉ TEMPLATES FOR A BUTTERFLY BLOCK

The following details are for making a butterfly appliqué, whether working by hand or machine, but the general method is the same whatever the shape.

Appliqué Worked by Hand

1   Plan your design on paper and number the appliqué shapes. Note which colors are to be used for each. For the butterfly block shown, you will need five different fabrics (diagram 1).

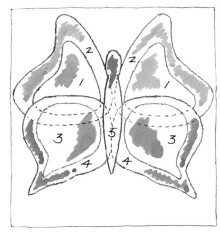

1

2   First trace the whole design, then using separate papers for each section, trace the shapes of the whole of the upper wing, the whole of the lower wing and the inner parts of both as well as the body (diagram 2).

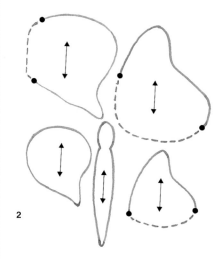

2

3   Templates for the righthand wings are shown here. As the butterfly is the same on both sides, you can save time by just cutting one template and turning it over to cut the mirror image. Mark this on your template.

4   Notice on the full design that the lower wings overlap the upper ones, so you do not need to neaten the edge of the underneath shapes. This saves work and bulk. Mark this area with dotted lines on the tracing, so you can transfer the marking to the fabric.

5   Note the direction of the straight of grain on each shape and cut out the templates.

Tip   *If you are only going to use the templates once, use the tracing paper, but if you will be using the motif several times, stick the tracings onto cardboard or template plastic and cut them out.*

6   Place each template on the right side of the chosen fabric and draw around with a marker. Mark the seam allowance: sometimes ¼in/0.75cm is too big for fiddly little shapes but if you are working in silk ¼in/0.75cm may not be enough to prevent it from fraying. Also mark any overlapping areas (diagram 3).

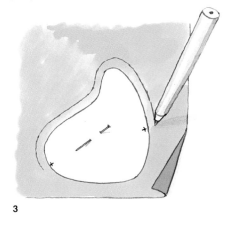

3

7   Mark out the design without seam allowances on the right side of your background fabric. A light box is helpful if you have one (see page 10).

8   Pin the first fabric piece in position, then use a needle to tuck under a short section of the seam allowance.

9   Hold the work with one hand and stitch with the other. Match the thread to the applied shape and work in slipstitch. Take small stitches and tuck the needle just under the shape to make them as invisible as possible (diagram 4).

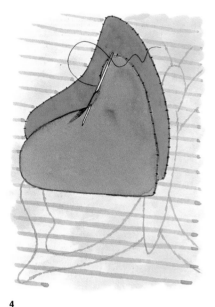

4

Appliqué Worked by Machine
I – Using Fusible Web

1   Plan the design as steps 1 and 2 above but instead of making paper templates, trace your design onto the paper side of the fusible web without seam allowances. Trace a mirror image if your design is not reversible. Mark the straight of the grain and the colors the shapes are to be cut from.

2   Cut out. Iron each shape onto the reverse of the chosen fabric. Cut out without seam allowances (diagram 5).

5

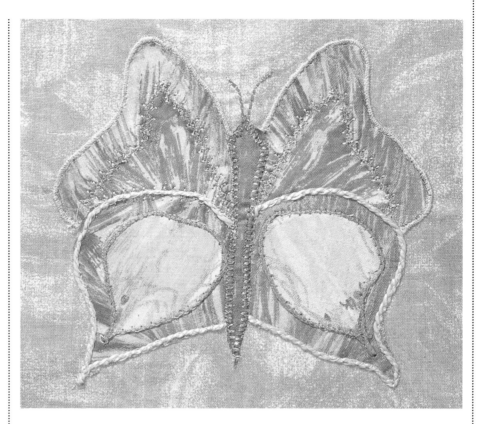

3   Carefully peel off the paper backing and use your original design to arrange the appliqué shapes on the background fabric.

4   Test the iron on some scraps of the fabrics you are using, then with the iron as hot as possible, bond the shapes to the background fabric.

5   Secure the edges with either a close zig-zag or a machine embroidery stitch. If you only have a straight stitch, stitch around each shape twice, then cover the edges with yarn, couched on by hand as shown in the photograph.

2 – Working from the Back

1   Trace or photocopy your design, in reverse, onto greaseproof or copy paper. Do not cut out.

2   Place the appliqué fabric, right side down, covered by the background fabric, right side down, and place the design on top. Pin and baste all the layers together.

3   Using a straight stitch and thread that matches the appliqué fabric, machine stitch over the lines of the drawing (diagram 6).

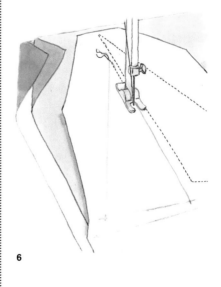

6

4   Leave the paper intact while you turn to the right side of the work. With sharp scissors, trim back the appliqué fabric close to the stitching, but outside the shape.

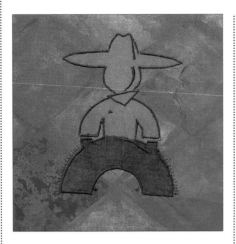

5 Secure the edges with a close zig-zag stitch, then tear away the paper from the reverse.

REVERSE APPLIQUÉ

This method uses two whole pieces of fabric for each layer. The upper fabric is cut away to reveal the one underneath. The method has several advantages over ordinary appliqué in certain circumstances, for example when irregular narrow shapes are needed or when the fabric you want to use for the motif is hard to manage, such as lamé or velvet.

Fabrics

For the upper layer, find a good-tempered fabric that will hold a fold from your finger pressing, such as a firm, lightweight cotton.

The under layer is less critical, in that you will only need to stitch into it, rather than make small turnings. A piece of tie-dyed or printed fabric, as used in the Rose Window Quilt on page 59, will often give an interesting effect. You can also use different fabrics for different motifs.

1 Plan the design on paper, then use a silver pencil or a blue pen to trace the design onto the right side of your upper fabric. A light box is helpful here, or you can tape the design and the fabric to the window to help you to see the line through the fabric.

2 Lay the under fabric, right side up, on the table. Carefully lower the upper fabric over the top, right side up, and smooth out any wrinkles. Pin, then baste the two layers of fabric together around the outer edges of the motifs.

3 The cutting and sewing of the design is done simultaneously. Use a sewing thread to match the upper layer. Work a slipstitch that shows hardly any thread on the top of the work but has a larger stitch showing on the reverse, making neat and evenly spaced stitches. Start on a simple part of the design and cut a slit of about 2in/5cm in the upper fabric only, about ³⁄₁₆in/3mm from the marked design line, on the motif side of the line.

4 Using the point of your needle, fold the upper fabric under as far as the design line. Stitch the upper fabric to the lower, with the design line on the fold (diagram 1). Keep cutting more of the design as you stitch.

1

5 If the design incorporates sharp points, such as the end of a narrow leaf, there will not be enough fabric for you to be able to make turnings in all directions. Cut cleanly to the point. Turn in what you can, then work extra stitches to secure the limited turning and raw edge (diagram 2).

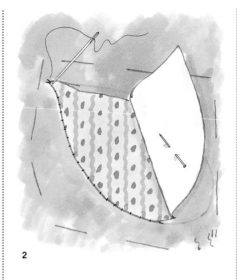

2

MOLA WORK

Mola work is an elaboration of the reverse appliqué technique. For this, several layers of different colored fabrics are used and cut into to expose tiny bands of different colors.

HAWAIIAN APPLIQUÉ

This term is used for a style of appliqué developed there in the middle of the 18th century. Designing and cutting out of the appliquéd piece (usually one shape to cover the whole quilt) follows the old idea of folding and cutting paper to make snowflake patterns.

The appliqué is slipstitched by hand, by turning in a small hem with the point of the needle as you go. The patterns are usually emphasized by using contour quilting – lines of quilting ½in/1.5cm apart – all around the shapes (see page 40).

BIAS STRIP APPLIQUÉ

This technique is sometimes referred to as "stained glass window" or "Celtic appliqué" but the common theme is that a strip of folded fabric, which has been cut on the bias, is used to make curves and to cover raw edges – either or both. Purchased bias binding can be used or there are other gadgets to help you achieve an even strip. The strips are usually stitched by hand but if you are a confident machinist, you might choose to use one of the utility stitches, such as the one that makes three straight stitches followed by one zig zag. Whichever way you choose, this is a style of appliqué that depends on good design and careful basting.

BRODERIE PERSE

For this type of appliqué, motifs are cut from a printed fabric and rearranged on a background fabric to make a new pattern. Its heyday was probably the 18th century when the oriental calicoes and chintzes caught the imagination of ladies who had plenty of time to spend on their work. The pieces of print are stitched onto the background – maybe a plain cotton or linen – without turning in the edges. This means that the edges need to be well stitched to avoid fraying. Many methods can be used, including couching a cord over the stitched edge to cover what is often unsightly but necessary stitching.

INLAY APPLIQUÉ

This style of appliqué is not often seen. As the name implies, it is made by fitting the appliqué shapes into holes that are the exact shape and size. The edges of both fabrics need to be secured in place and prevented from fraying. In the sample shown, I have used a modern fabric that does not fray – a lightweight matt velour.

Lay the two fabrics on top of each other, right way up. Place your appliqué template on top and, using a sharp craft knife, cut through both fabrics at the same time, so that the shapes are exactly the same. Separate them carefully (if you wish you can work two pieces of appliqué – in a "robbing Peter to pay Paul" manner).

Place the motif of one color into the hole of the other color and stitch, using a utility stitch that catches in both motif and background at the same time. To give additional strength, both pieces can be ironed onto lightweight iron-on interfacing before stitching.

Sailboats Bed Quilt

THIS BRIGHTLY COLORED QUILT, APPLIQUÉD BY MACHINE, IS IDEAL FOR AN OLDER CHILD'S SINGLE BED. ALL THE APPLIQUÉ SHAPES ARE CUT FROM THE SAME LARGE PRINT CHECK. THE ANCHORS ARE CUT FROM THE SAME AREA OF THE DESIGN EACH TIME, WHEREAS THE SAILBOATS ARE CUT AT RANDOM, THUS COMBINING UNIFORMITY AND CHANCE WITH A HAPPY RESULT.

Quilt size: 68in x 96/173 x 244cm

Materials

All the fabrics used in the quilt are cotton and 45in/115cm wide

◘ Anchor block backgrounds and inner border: 2½yards/2.25m textured print

◘ Filler blocks, outer border and piping: 2¾yards/2.5m coordinating stripe

◘ Sailboat block backgrounds: 3yards/2.5m textured print

◘ Sailboats: 2½yards/2.25m large print – to ensure variety

◘ Anchors: 1½yards/1.25m solid color

◘ Backing: 5⅔yards/5.1m

◘ Piping: 10yards/9m of 5mm cord

◘ Batting: 2oz polyester, 72 x 100in/183 x 254cm (two pieces joined if necessary)

◘ Invisible machine quilting thread

CUTTING

1   For the inner border, cut two strips, 4½ x 84½in/11.5 x 214.5cm, and two strips 4½ x 64½in/11.5 x 164cm.

2   For the outer border, cut two strips, 2½ x 92½in/6 x 235cm, and two strips, 2½ x 68½in/6 x 174cm.

3   For the piping, cut strips 2in/5cm wide to a total length of 340in/860cm using the same fabric as the outer border. I cut the fabric on the bias, so that it showed diagonal stripes on the piping, to resemble a rope.

4   For the background to the boats, cut 25 pieces, 10 x 13in/33 x 25cm.

5   For the background to the anchors, cut 24 squares, 10 x 10in/25 x 25cm.

6   For the filler blocks, cut 24 pieces, 4 x 10in/10 x 25cm.

7   For the sailboats, cut 25 pieces, 9 x 12in/23 x 30.5cm.

8   For the anchors, cut 24 squares, 8 x 8in/20.5 x 20.5cm, using the same area of pattern for each piece.

9   Cut the backing fabric in half horizontally and, taking a 1in/2.5cm seam, join to make one piece, 72 x 100in/183 x 254cm. Remove the selvages and press the seam open.

10   Following the templates on page 57, make and cut 25 photocopies or tracings of the full-size sailboat and 24 copies of the full-size anchor.

MAKING THE APPLIQUÉ BLOCKS

1   Following the instructions given for "working from the back" (see page 51), place a piece of sailboat fabric on the work surface, right side down, and cover with a piece of sailboat background fabric, right side down. Place a tracing of the sailboat on top and stitch the sailboat design.

2   Cut around the applied shape from the front, then stitch using a close zig-zag stitch (diagram 1). Remove the papers. Repeat to make 25 blocks.

1

3   Repeat steps 1 and 2 to make 24 anchor blocks. Press all the blocks.

4   With right sides together, stitch a filler block to the base of each anchor block as shown in the quilt assembly plan. Press the seams open.

5   Trim all the blocks to measure 12½ x 9½in/32 x 24cm.

ASSEMBLING THE BLOCKS

1   Taking a ¼in/0.75cm seam, make up the rows of alternate blocks: four with four sailboats and three anchors and three with three sailboats and four anchors (diagram 2). Press the seams open.

2   Stitch the rows together, starting with a row containing four sailboats and joining onto it one with four anchors (diagram 3). Continue with the alternating pattern until all the rows have been stitched together. Press.

2

3

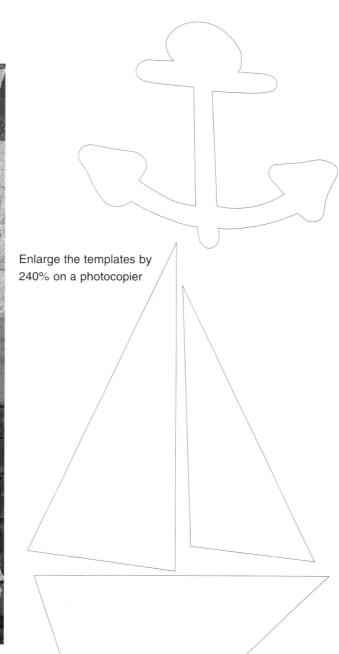

Enlarge the templates by
240% on a photocopier

ADDING THE BORDERS AND PIPING

1   Stitch the side inner borders to the pieced top, taking a ¼in/0.75cm seam.

2   Stitch the top and bottom inner borders to the pieced top and borders.

3   Stitch the side outer borders to the pieced top and inner borders.

4   Stitch the top and bottom outer borders to the pieced top and borders.

5   Prepare the piping (see page 74). You will need to join strips together to make a total length of roughly 335in/850cm.

6   Attach the piping to the pieced top around the edges with the raw edges aligned with the borders. Press the seams to the back of the pieced top, so that the piping sits on the edge.

FINISHING

1   Lay out the backing piece, right side down. Cover this with the batting. Carefully center the quilt top,

right side up, over the batting and use safety pins, placed at least four in each block, to hold the layers together.

2   Choose one of the methods described on pages 39 to 41 to machine-quilt. I chose to stitch horizontal wavy lines across the quilt, using the utility stitch recommended for stitching on elastic, extended as wide and as long as possible.

3   Turn under the raw edges of the backing. Slipstitch to the piping on the back of the quilt, enclosing the batting.

Rose Window Wall Quilt

ALTHOUGH THE INSPIRATION FOR THIS QUILT COMES FROM MEDIAEVAL ROSE WINDOWS IN CHURCHES AND

CATHEDRALS, THE FINISHED PIECE IS NOT MEANT TO BE A DIRECT REPRESENTATION.

THE QUILT IS WORKED IN REVERSE APPLIQUÉ (SEE PAGE 52).

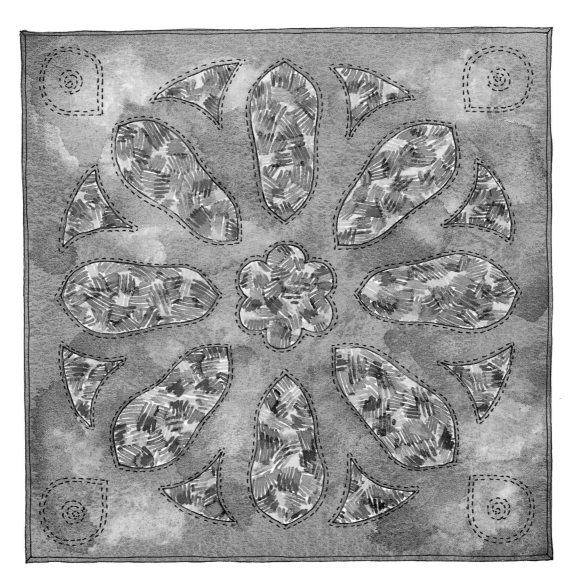

Quilt size: 40 x 40in/101.5 x 101.5cm

Materials

All fabrics used in the patchwork top are 45in/115cm wide.

- ▣ Stone surface: 1½yards/1.25m textured effect print or hand dyed cotton in a neutral color
- ▣ Background: 1½yards/1.25m brightly colored print
- ▣ Sewing thread to match stone fabric

- ▣ Backing and sleeve: 1½yards/1.25m
- ▣ Batting: 42in/107cm square
- ▣ Binding: 5½yards/5m purchased bias binding to match background fabric
- ▣ Doweling to hang the quilt

PREPARING THE PATTERN

1   On the right side of the neutral stone fabric baste lines to mark the outside dimensions of the quilt, 40 x 40in/101.5 x 101.5cm, then baste lines to make two crosses (diagram 1).

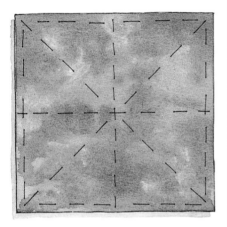

1

2   Trace the templates given on page 61 and cut out in cardboard.

3   Following the quilt assembly plan, place the petal shapes along the lines of the basted crosses, aligning the center line with the line of basting. The smaller end of each petal shape is placed 6in/15cm from the center (diagram 2). Use a marker pencil to draw around the templates.

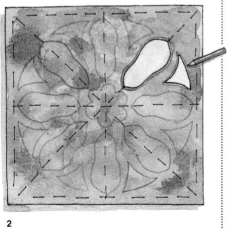

2

4   Center a triangular template between each petal, with the inner point 14in/35.5cm from the center. Draw around as before.

5   Place the flower shape in the center. Draw around.

6   Lay out the background print fabric on a flat surface, right side up, and smooth it out. Cover it with the marked neutral fabric, also right side up, and baste together ½in/1.5cm outside the design lines of the motifs.

STITCHING

1   Following the instructions for reverse appliqué (see page 52), cut away a little of the neutral fabric from the motif side of one of the petal shapes. Tuck under the seam allowance up to the design line and slipstitch to the underneath fabric, using a thread to match the upper fabric.

2   Continue in this way until all the motifs have been exposed.

3   Press the quilt top carefully and cut away the excess print fabric from the reverse to save bulk.

FINISHING

1   From the backing fabric, cut a piece, 42in/107cm square. Lay out, right side down, and cover with the

batting. Carefully center the appliquéd top, right side up, over the batting and baste the three layers together in a grid formation.

2   Hand-quilt (see page 37) to give the impression of the lead between the stained glass and designs carved in the stonework (diagram 3).

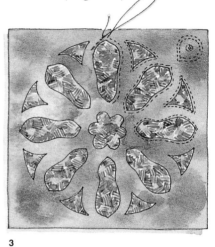

3

3   Using the purchased binding, bind the quilt, cutting off the excess batting and reverse fabric as you go.

4   Make a sleeve for the reverse of the quilt (see page 23), thread through the length of doweling and hang.

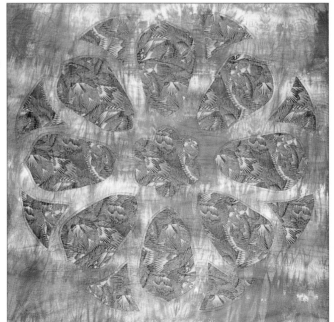

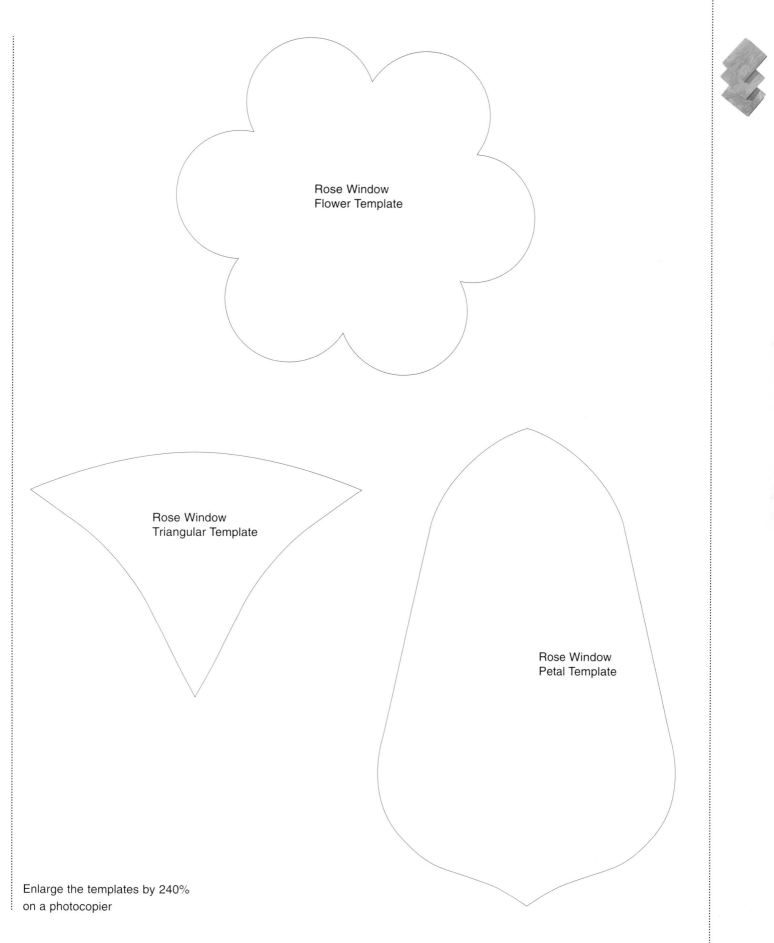

Rose Window
Flower Template

Rose Window
Triangular Template

Rose Window
Petal Template

Enlarge the templates by 240%
on a photocopier

DESIGNING A QUILT

I would like to encourage everyone to design their own quilts and I hope to help with suggestions for some easy steps here. To begin with, try everything. Join a group, go to day schools, share your learning with others, read books and magazines to develop an understanding of the tremendously wide range of possibilities there are in quiltmaking. Attend exhibitions to see what other quiltmakers are doing and to see what's new in fabrics and useful gadgets.

Designing is about choosing. Most of us are very experienced choosers – what to wear, what to buy, what to eat. Have the courage to transfer this skill to quiltmaking.

FINDING A DESIGN
People often ask me, "Where do you get your ideas from?" Nowadays, I have lots of ideas, but it was not always so. I had to become tuned in to pattern and design. I collect design ideas all the time from many different sources:

◆ I cut out pictures from Sunday supplements, from greetings cards and from advertising brochures and stick them randomly into a scrap book.
◆ I carry a notebook and write down ideas as I come across them – maybe for a color scheme. I draw architectural motifs and the way tiles are laid to make a pattern – just note-taking drawings.
◆ I take photographs of things I like – gates, flower beds, trees, fungi, walls, reflections, floors.

These are all there for inspiration: some of them will never be used.

So now I can assume that you have learned some techniques and collected some design ideas.
◆ Start with something you like: perhaps a technique you enjoy or a quilt you've already made. It may be

that when you have made the sailboat quilt you will feel confident to use the motifs in your own way – make copies of the sailboat motif in different sizes and arrange five or six sailboats in a seascape for a wall hanging or place six or seven smaller anchors in a circle for a cushion. Perhaps one of the fabric manipulation techniques could be used alone for a cushion, using your own hand-dyed fabric.
◆ Think about what kind of design the technique is best suited to. Look through your ideas collection and try to find three possibilities. Write a note to yourself about each one, describing what you like about it. You might like to add some thoughts about how it would work in a quilt.
◆ How big do you want your finished quilt to be – a bed quilt, a lap quilt, a hanging? Consider each of your three possibilities. Is there enough detail in the design for the size you need – perhaps you could repeat the pattern. Or maybe there is too much detail – it is too complicated – can it be simplified or should you just work on a small section?

Now that you have decided on a size and a design, draw it up to scale (see page 65) to fill a sheet of paper: this is just a first impression and is concerned with looking at the spatial relations of the different parts.

Leave it for a while, then take another look. Does it still please you or would a border, or several borders, help? Will the parts that require most work be placed where they will be most obvious?

Draw it out again to see if it can be improved. Tracing paper and photocopies can be a great help and if you are happier cutting than drawing, make a collage of cut paper or fabric.

Now do some sampling. You need to

work at the intended finished size. Choose a small section – say a block and make your templates as described on page 50 for appliqué shapes or page 68 for patchwork blocks. Make a sample of the section in the way that you have planned and consider whether it will work.

Take your time deciding, go and do something else and try to keep taking a glance at the work. If you have a reducing glass, take a long distance look. If it doesn't seem quite right, make some small changes. Often color schemes are too bland and need to have just a small quantity of a sharp contrast fabric added.

USING THE COMPUTER
If you want to make a quilt from blocks and have access to a computer with the right sort of program, you will be able to design your own block design, then create secondary patterns by grouping, rotating and stepping it (diagram 1).

You can also experiment with the effects of different colors and densities of color. Look at the diagrams of the Texas star block (diagram 2) to see the difference that is made when the weight of color is changed. Making comparisons such as this takes only minutes on the computer.

Likewise, experimenting with a design for a quilt which uses more than one block can be speeded up considerably if you can use a computer to work out the variations (diagram 3).

Some drawing packages will suffice but there are also special patchwork programs which are fascinating to use. I have even been warned about the trap of spending all the time available working out designs so that there's no time left to stitch.

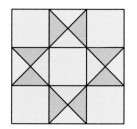

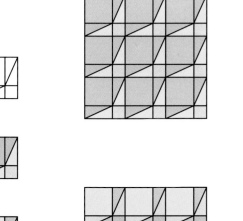

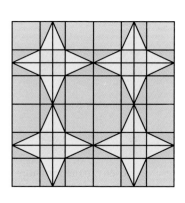

1

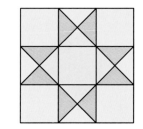

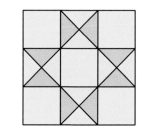

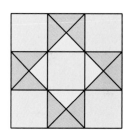

2

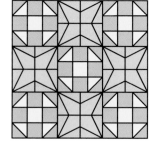

3

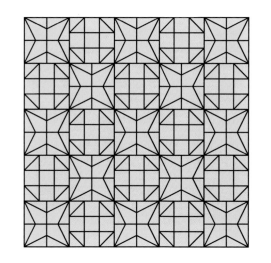

COLOR

You will find it helpful to refer to books about color theory when you feel that you want to be more adventurous with color, but I am including some simple theory here. Do not be daunted by the thought of theory. Look at the color wheel (diagram 1) and make one for yourself, using paints, pastels or crayons that you can blend together. The simple one-ring wheel starts with the three primary colors:

yellow
red
blue

1

In between these there are other colors that are formed by mixing the primary colors. You will remember that when you mix yellow and blue you make green, orange comes from red and yellow, and violet from red and blue. On the wheel, you will find them midway between the primaries that contribute to them. They are referred to as secondary colors:

orange
violet
green

The mixing together of a primary and a secondary color gives us a further range of colors, the tertiaries:

yellow-orange
red-orange
red-violet
blue-violet
blue-green
yellow-green

On the wheel they come between the primary and the secondary colors.

When you come to try to match fabrics and threads to these colors you may find that color seems much more complicated, so try mixing a little black with each of the colors and find the related darker color: these are referred to as tones. Then repeat the experiment with white and make tints. Even so, there will be some fabric colors you cannot match and these can be thought of as "greyed". There are so many colors that we would think of as grey and so the concept of grey in itself is not straightforward. Nevertheless, every grey is made up of a selection of the colors already mentioned and mixing grey with another color will dull it, without necessarily making it darker (a tone) or lighter (a tint). Try it for yourself. Use your coloring materials and try to recreate the color of a fabric that you think is "greyed".

The other aspect of color you may like to consider is the question of saturation. Think of a red chiffon scarf. When folded into 64 the color you see is a saturated red. Open it up and the color is much less clear – not a tint, as if you had mixed white with the red – just less strong. This is something that

you need to be aware of when you experiment with dyeing.

So let us return to the color wheel. We often use the term complementary colors. This term refers to any two colors that are directly opposite to each other on the wheel: yellow and violet, blue and orange. The contrast is at its strongest with such a scheme and using equal quantities of two such colors is dramatic but sometimes defeats the object because the colors fight for dominance and confuse the eye. If you want to make a two-color composition using complementaries, make sure that there is a lot more of one than the other. Try it out with paper cut from magazines if you are reluctant to use fabric to experiment.

A useful way to use the concept of complementary colors is to cut some cardboard into a triangular shape to fit exactly over a segment of the color wheel (diagram 2).

2

Place it across the color wheel so that the curve lies on the outside of the wheel and the triangle covers a whole segment. The sharp point of the triangle will point to a color that is complementary to the covered segment. Match up three fabrics to this selection, i.e. one on either side of the triangle and the one pointed to, you will find that the colors work well together.

If you do not feel quite so brave, try selecting three colors that sit next to each other on the wheel. This will often give you a strong color scheme that will fit into a number of different room settings. The word used for this style of color scheme is analogous.

I have made a number of patchwork projects using monochromatic color schemes, i.e. based on one color only. Often I have used my own dyed fabrics for this, which gave me confidence that the fabrics would all match, but the range of fabrics available is wide enough for you to be able to select. This time you will need to find fabrics where the color is mixed with black and with white and where the saturation varies. Using fabrics with different fiber content and different weaves are all helpful in creating variety in such a scheme.

Some of my most dramatic work has not used color at all, depending on either just black, just white or just black and white.

ENLARGING A DESIGN
Patchwork Blocks

Enlarging geometric patchwork blocks is easily done by drawing the larger shape on graph or isometric paper.

Freehand designs

To demonstrate the method for enlarging a freehand design, I've used the example of the book cover which I enlarged to make my "Blue Vine" quilt and I've worked only in inches to simplify the maths.

1   Decide how big the quilt is going to be. (I wanted to make a cover, 108 x 108in, for a four-poster bed but the design did not need to go right to the edges of the quilt.)

2   Take account of the proportion of the height to the width. (I thought that if the width was the same as the bed (54in), there would be room for the height of the design to run over the bottom of the bed.)

3   To find this proportion or, in other words, the width/height ratio, measure the original source (in my case, the book cover was 4.25 x 6.6in).

4   Using a calculator, key in the larger figure (6.6) and divide it by the smaller (4.25). The result, 1.56 – near enough one and a half – is the ratio.

5   Take the width of the design area for the quilt, 54in, and multiply it by 1.56 (the ratio), which gives 83.7in. This gives the depth of the finished design. I wanted to have some space above and below the design on the quilt so I centered it, leaving 12in at both top and bottom.

6   Take a tracing of the major shapes of the original design. Mine was a rubbing, as the book cover was embossed.

7   Trim the tracing paper so that the edges of the paper are the edges of the design.

8   Fold the paper accurately into four lengthways, then again so that there are eight vertical divisions across the top. Fold the paper into eight crossways, so that you have 64 rectangles. Mark the folds with pencil lines, then write numbers 1 to 8 down one side and letters A to H across the bottom, so that each square will have its own reference (diagram 1). This is the design.

9   Make up a sheet of paper as large as your quilt by overlapping and sticking sheets of paper together. Make it exact with no spare around the edges. Fold the paper to make 64 divisions as described above and mark the rows of rectangles 1 to 8 and A to H in the same way. This is the pattern.

10   Working on one rectangle at a time draw what appears on the design onto your pattern. You will find that it is not nearly so daunting when you have just a small portion to draw. Use a soft pencil, something like a 2B lead, and have an eraser handy. Note where

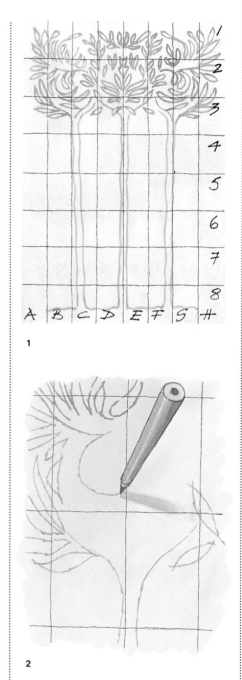

the lines cross the grid and how much of each square is taken up by the pattern (diagram 2).

11   When all the rectangles are completed you will have your pattern. At this stage, you may want to take a tracing of it so that you can cut it up to use for templates.

PLANNING A QUILT

FABRIC CHOICE
For patchwork

100% cotton: Many quiltmakers always choose to use the American cotton fabrics we have come to associate with patchwork. They are light in weight, sufficiently closely woven as not to fray easily, making the usual ¼in/0.75cm seam practicable, they hold a crease and generally do what is asked of them. I would certainly recommend them for a beginner. The choice of prints and solids is overwhelming and you can usually buy "fat quarters" (measuring 18 x 22in or when a metre of 115cm wide fabric is divided into four "almost squares"), which means that you can collect a good selection of patterns and colors without great expense.

Scraps: Others prefer to follow the tradition of quiltmaking as an economy art and use scraps from dressmaking, remnants from sales and even rummage sale finds. I am all in favour of this in our throw-away society, but there are some pitfalls. If you are making patchwork, it is easier if the fabrics are similar to each other in fiber content and weight. When using former items of clothing, discard any parts that are showing even a hint of wear. If you intend to quilt the patchwork by hand, use only the lighter weight fabrics.

Challenging fabrics: While I would advise beginners to steer away from knits, satins and velvets, these fabrics can lend great excitement to a quilt. Sometimes, when I have wanted "just that color" and the fabric was not what I would normally count as a patchwork fabric, I have had to devise ways to use it.

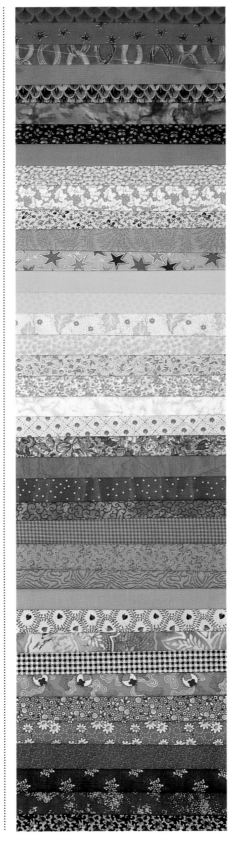

Solutions to Challenging Fabrics

◆ they are too slippery – use plenty of pins and close basting, possibly both, or stiffen them temporarily with freezer paper.
◆ they are too heavy – strengthen the adjoining fabrics with interfacing or fabric manipulation, or temporarily with paper.
◆ they are too flimsy – strengthen them with interfacing or fabric manipulation, by layering or embroidery, or temporarily with paper.
◆ they are too floppy – stabilize them with interfacing or spray starch or with one of the stabilizing effects above.
◆ they are too stretchy – stabilize as for the fabrics that are too floppy if you need to but try to use knits creatively in terms of fabric manipulation.
◆ they move in ways of their own (these as usually the ones with a pile) – try using pins and basting, and if stitching by machine, an evenfeed foot.

Using Challenging Fabrics

Having looked at so many negatives, consider the positives. Work samples to explore the different possibilities that these out-of-the-ordinary fabrics give:
◆ use different colors of the same sort of fabric;
◆ use different fabrics together – firm to floppy;
◆ try stitching chiffon to a knit, stretching the knit as you go;
◆ machine densely into the pile of velvet in some parts, leaving other areas untouched;
◆ trap threads or scraps of lurex in between layers of transparent fabric;
◆ experiment to discover whether it is best if the pile of one piece is running in the same direction or in the opposite direction to that of its neighbour. Check to see what visual effects you can create by the differences in pile.

Silk: Some patchworkers choose only to work in silk because the results are so wonderful. Again, you must take the weight of the fabric into consideration – there is a great variety. Either work this into the design of your quilt or use one of the methods above for equalizing the weights. Silk also frays easily, so that the usual seam allowance (¼in/0.75cm) may not be sufficient. Do some sampling, using the exact silk that you have chosen, before you cut out the majority of your patches.

Wool: In Wales there is a tradition of using woollen fabrics for patchwork, often dressmaking remnants or the good bits remaining from worn-out clothes. Take care to choose fabrics of a similar weight, but you will not find problems of slippery surfaces and fraying and it is easy to stitch by hand.

Patterns, prints and stripes: Some years ago the majority of American cottons available were small prints. These are the very best choice if you want to camouflage seams and some blocks depend on the eye being thus deceived.

Plains, or "solids", have been less popular but the clarity of the colors often recommends them and they are the first choice for Amish-style quilts.

During the last ten years we have seen the introduction of large prints. Some of these have dramatic color schemes and, if you find one you like, it can provide a good starting point for your fabric selection. Use it as your focus fabric and find a mixture of small prints and solids to complement it. The way that different parts of the large print appear at random gives a lively feel to the work.

Look, too, for the newer fashion of texture-look prints, tie-dye and space-dye effects, which serve as small prints without confusing the color scheme.

Your local quilters' supplies shop will also be able to offer you a wide range of theme fabrics: fishing and golf for Dad, music for the teenagers, space men for the school children and nursery motifs for the youngest. You can cut such prints at random, offering a lively chance result, or you can cut them carefully and arrange them to form their own pattern in the piecing (see page 45 on using window templates for this purpose).

Stripes, too, have their own special uses and, once again there is a great

variety, from simple candy stripes to elaborate patterned stripes such as you find on wall paper and furnishing fabrics. Quiltmakers cut these into long strips to use for borders and they can be very effective (see page 55).

There has been a great interest in the use of stripes and checks in reproducing the character of traditional workaday quilts made from shirting offcuts. The texture of these prints often feels different from the usual prints, representing the different intended use for the original fabric, and the colors are often muted – sensitive to what used to be regarded as male color schemes. It is difficult to arrange for the lines of such stripes and checks to align accurately, so, if accuracy is not your forte, before embarking on a project like this, make some samples to see how you like them. Many people would see a "hit and miss" effect as attractive but you might find it uncomfortable.

For Appliqué

For the traditional hand appliqué, which depends on turning under a small seam allowance and holding it in place while you stitch it, the majority of the comments I have made above apply. However, it is possible to be more adventurous when using either of the machine appliqué methods described on page 51. This is particularly useful when you are trying to interpret a picture and the mixture of fabrics will add interest to the piece. If the work will need to be laundered, beware of using fabrics that might react differently from each other when in the wash or when being ironed.

For Backing

Quilts can be backed with plain fine cotton, such as muslin, or with a patterned fabric which complements the quilt top. If a quilt is to be hand-quilted, it's important to choose a backing fabric which is easy to pass a needle through.

FABRIC PREPARATION

Many patchworkers like to wash fabric before use to ensure that if it is going to shrink, run or fade, it will not spoil their quilt. Another advantage of doing this is that, when ironing the washed fabric, you can ensure that the grain is true. Personally, I like to work with crisp material, so I do not wash it unless it is dirty or if I am dyeing it. For wallhangings that are unlikely to be washed, you can afford to take risks.

TEMPLATES

Templates are the patterns that you draw and cut around to make sure that your patchwork fits together. It is important for them to be accurate. For hundreds of years quiltmakers have made their own and many people still do this, but you can now purchase professionally made templates for many of the popular shapes, and at least one firm offers sets of templates for well-loved blocks.

For Cutting or Stitching

Depending on the sort of work you are doing, you may need either a cutting template or a stitching template or both. For traditional hexagons, for example, you need a template the size of the finished patch (for the papers) and a template with seam allowances (for cutting the fabric). To choose particular sections of a print fabric, use a transparent template (see page 45).

Pressing Templates

It can be useful, especially when fabrics are cut on the bias, to draw the exact shape of the pieced section on a sheet of paper to have on the ironing board and check against, in order to avoid distorting the fabric as you press it.

Making Your Own Templates

If you decide to make your own templates, you need to think of ways to help you to be accurate – for example, use a hard pencil rather than a soft one

and cut with a craft knife and a board rather than scissors. You may find it helpful to draw onto graph paper – you can buy both imperial and metric grids. Another useful grid is isometric, which gives 30 and 60 degree angles instead

of right angles. Cardboard can be used but template plastic will not wear so quickly; is also semi-transparent. Do test your template before you cut out too much fabric.

If you have access to a computer, you may be able to use it to draw exact lengths and angles. You can use it to print papers for English patchwork because the shapes are easily duplicated.

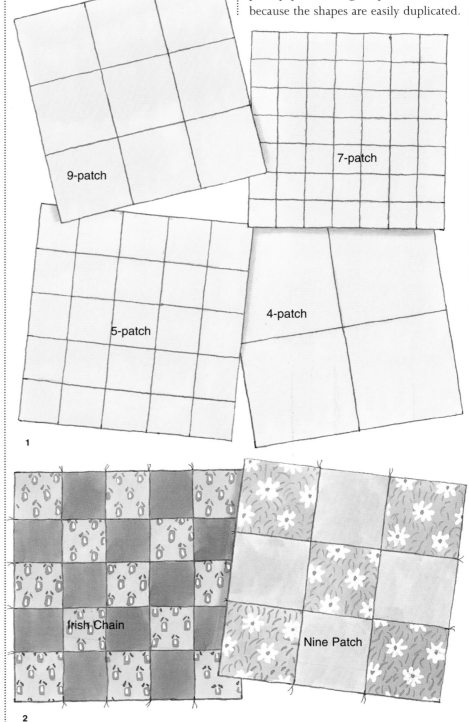

9-patch

7-patch

5-patch

4-patch

1

Irish Chain

Nine Patch

2

DRAFTING REGULAR BLOCKS

Blocks are grouped according to the underlying grid of squares on which the pattern is based, rather than the number of pieces of fabric. They are described as 4-patch, 5-patch, 7-patch and 9-patch (diagram 1).

These basic grids can be further divided to make a large number of classic blocks, but two of the simplest but nonetheless effective blocks use an undivided grid: "Nine Patch" and "Irish Chain". They depend for their effect on color placement (diagram 2).

To draft blocks simply use graph paper. The following examples give some basic methods as a start for your own experiments.

1 *Snowball*: Decide on the size of the block: 7½in/18cm is a good size for this design. It is not necessary to draft a pattern for the nine patch as the nine squares are all 2½in/6cm. For the snowball, draw a square 7½ x 7½in/ 18 x 18cm and make marks on the edge to divide each side into three equal parts of 2½in/6cm. Join the marks on the adjacent sides to make the four small triangles (diagram 3).

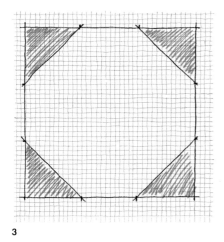

3

2 *Shoo Fly* is also based on a nine-patch block. To draft this block, follow the same procedure to draw the triangles, then join the marks to make the grid of nine squares (diagram 4).

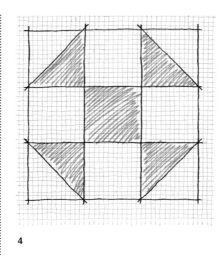

4

3 *Windmill* is a four-patch block using two sizes of triangles. Draw a square, say 8 x 8in/20 x 20cm, and divide it into four equal squares. Draw a diagonal cross in each of these squares, then following diagram 5 (which shows four blocks) disregard one line in each square to color in the triangles that you will piece.

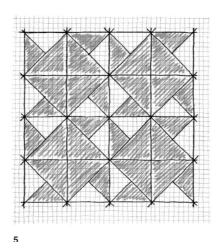

5

Using Mirrors

Planning a quilt that uses blocks can be fascinating. First color in some graph paper to make a couple of sample blocks, then place hinged mirrors (see page 10) on the edges of your block design, to obtain repeat images. Often the secondary patterns that are reflected in the mirrors where four blocks join are as interesting as the blocks you planned.

DRAWING SHAPES WITHOUT A PROTRACTOR

Pioneer women crossing the prairies often relied on folding up pieces of paper and using the resultant shapes for their templates. Try this for yourself.

1 Use crisp paper that will fold into sharp creases. Take a right angled corner (A) as your starting point and measure the same distance in two directions (to B and D), see diagram 1.

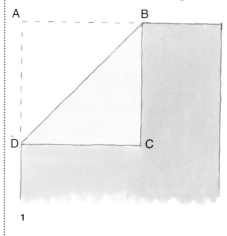

1

2 Fold over the corner A along the diagonal from B to D and make point C. Join up the points. You now have a good square and can cut it out.

3 You can fold this square in different ways to form different blocks. For example, fold it in half, then diagonally and mix with plain squares to make the Texas Star block (diagram 2).

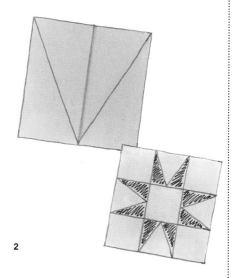

2

4 Or it can be folded into four squares and diagonally, then used in groups of four to make the four pointed star (diagram 3).

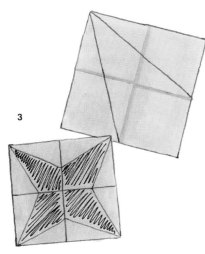

3

DRAWING SHAPES WITH A PROTRACTOR

In order for regular shapes to fit together, or tessellate, which is essential for a patchwork, their angles need to add up to 360°. Thus four squares will fit together because their angles are all 90°. Four diamond shapes will fit in the 360°, provided their sharp points are 60°, and their other angles 120°. The angles of hexagons are all 120°, so only three are needed to make up the 360°. Equilateral triangles have 60° angles so it takes six for them to fit together around a point. These shapes all have sides of equal lengths but the principle of 360° holds true however you make up the center (diagram 4).

Use the protractor to check angles and to create geometric templates. To prepare a drawing of a triangle with a 20° point and two equal sides, draw the base line the required length and measure angles of 80° at each end of the line with the protractor. Draw lines from the base line through the 80° mark on both sides and continue until they meet: the angle obtained will be 20° (diagram 5). The same drawing process can be used for any such triangle required.

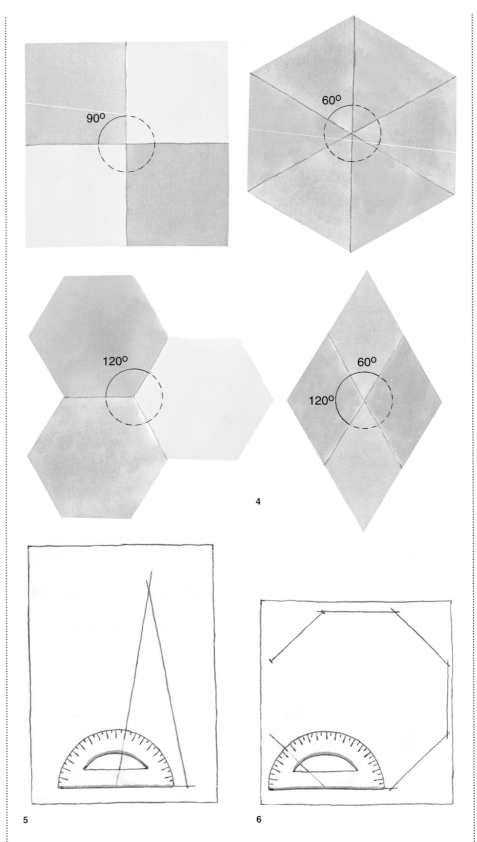

4

5

6

To draw an octagon, start with a base line of the required length and using your protractor, draw angles measuring

135° at each end. Continue these lines. Mark off the length of the base line and measure another 135° angle. Continue

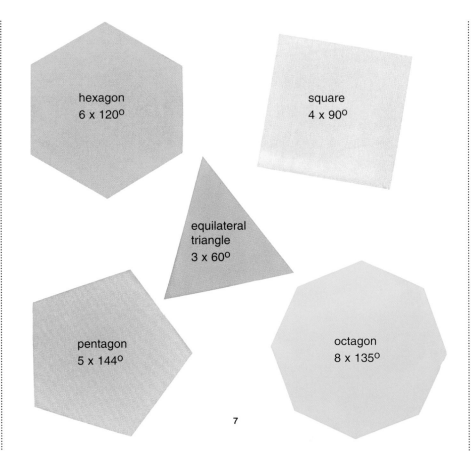

hexagon
6 x 120°

square
4 x 90°

equilateral
triangle
3 x 60°

pentagon
5 x 144°

octagon
8 x 135°

7

Pay attention to the grain requirements, whether the templates need to be flipped to give mirror images, whether you are matching patterns and to the seam allowances needed. Do not plan to use the last ½in/2cm of the width of the fabric: sometimes there is a slight variation or a wide selvage.

Tip *Remember not to use the selvage – its composition may well be different from the rest of the fabric and thus may spoil your quilt.*

2   Measure the fabric for each color in the block, multiply by the number of blocks or appliqué shapes needed and add an extra 10% as a precaution. This will give the amount for the pieced top. The borders may be in one of the block colors or a contrasting one.

Note the following:
◆ If you are using fat quarters, you may find that they do not work out quite so economically as using the full width of the fabric.

◆ Another trap is associated with narrow angles, such as you find at the sharp end of diamonds. They can sometimes be quite greedy with fabric when you take into account the seam allowances, so plan carefully.

◆ If you need long pieces of fabric for the borders, allow for this when planning your fabric purchase. It is considered acceptable to join the fabric for the border, but if this can be avoided, I think it is worth the effort. The "Sailboats" quilt on page 49 has simple borders using the same fabrics that are used in the blocks. The quantity needed is such that the full width of fabric rather than fat quarters is appropriate, but, even so, the borders must be cut first to avoid seams.

in this way until the last two sides meet at an angle of 135° (diagram 6).

The angles required for the various common shapes are shown in diagram 7. The method of measuring lines and angles is the same as given above.

Making Appliqué Templates
To make irregular shapes for appliqué, follow the instructions on page 50.

HOW MUCH MATERIAL DO YOU NEED FOR YOUR QUILT?
This is a source of great concern to some quiltmakers. The fabrics you choose may be costly, so you do not want to buy more than necessary. On the other hand, if you are using a very simple palette, it would be disastrous to run out of one of the fabrics.

Many of the specialist shops selling fabric for quilting are staffed by quilters who are willing to help you choose and to give advice. I would always want

to err on the side of caution feeling that, as I like the fabric anyway, I shall be happy to use up any leftovers in another quilt. Some designs, such as those giving a 3D effect, as in the "Attic Windows" quilt on page 117, are dependent on having exactly the right fabric. It may be that you intend to dye your own cotton in order to obtain a precise gradation – be sure to dye enough.

There is a fashion currently for using a series of fabrics which, from a distance, give the same overall effect. This can take some of the worry out of calculations. You should be able to find more of at least one of the fabrics you are using, if needed.

1   When you have prepared the templates, cut a few shapes in paper or waste fabric and place them economically on a piece of fabric of the width you intend to buy. Do this for each of the colors you intend to use.

SURFACE TREATMENTS
Dyeing

If you have not tried dyeing fabric, then you may be missing an excellent opportunity for self expression: do try some, at least once. There is a variety of reasons for dyeing: to obtain a specific color, to obtain a greater variety of shades, to change the color of a piece of fabric that you don't like, in order to make use of it.

Dyes

Start with two colors of cold water dyes. Choose colors that you think work well together.

Utensils

Find some utensils that you can keep just for dyeing, because the dyes are chemicals that you need to treat with respect. You will need:
◆ two large plastic containers, such as ice cream containers or old washing-up bowls
◆ a stick or old-fashioned washing tongs
◆ jam jars
◆ spoons

Other requirements:
◆ kitchen salt
◆ running water and a sink
◆ washing powder
◆ a waterproof apron, rubber gloves and a mask for when you are handling the dry powder

Fabrics

Natural fibers accept the dye best, so start with cotton. Use a variety of fabrics, such as calico, muslin, sheeting and poplin, with, perhaps, some prints or woven designs and stripes. You can put in some polycotton mixtures if you wish, but they will come out paler. Use small pieces of experimental fabrics, fat quarters and even larger pieces of calico or sheeting. Weigh the dry fabrics and use the quantities of dye and salt stated in the manufacturer's instructions.

Plain Dyeing, Tie-dyeing and Two-color Dyeing

1   Take two pieces of fabric for tie-dyeing. There are many ways to prepare fabric for tie-dyeing but I find the simplest is to tie knots in the fabric. Pull as hard as you can so that the dye cannot penetrate the inside of the knot.

2   Soak the remainder of the fabric pieces thoroughly in cold water for a couple of hours.

3   Prepare two dye baths, one for each color, following the manufacturer's instructions.

4   Reserve one piece of wet fabric and wring out the rest. Divide the dry, tied-up fabrics and the remaining wrung-out fabrics between the two dye baths and leave them for the time stated in the instructions, agitating frequently to ensure that the dye penetrates evenly.

5   Wearing rubber gloves, remove the fabrics with a stick or tongs.

6   Draw the two dye baths close together. Take the reserved piece of wet fabric and place part in one dye and part in the other. The two dyes should seep into the area that is not submerged and merge to give a third color.

7   While the two-colored piece is absorbing the dye, work with one color at a time and place the fabrics in the kitchen sink, leaving aside the tie-dyed pieces. Run cold water over the dyed fabric until it runs clear. This seems to take ages. Remove when clear.

8   Now repeat with the tie-dyed pieces. When the water is clear, remove and untie the knots, then rinse again, in case some dye is still trapped.

9   Finally, rinse the two-colored piece separately, in the same way.

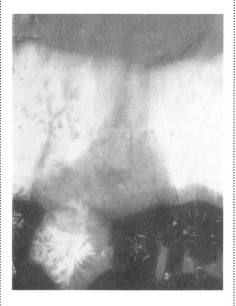

10   Wash the fabrics thoroughly in hot soapy water – in the washing machine if you wish. Dry and iron your fabrics and admire the results.

Using Dyed Fabrics

Because you have made such a good job of rinsing and washing, you will be able to use your dyed fabrics with others if you wish. You will find that the tie-dyed fabric and the two-colored one give you additional scope. Stitching a series of log cabin blocks or using the dyed shades for appliquéd flower petals can make a piece of work that is very much your own.

PRINTING

Printing can be great fun and it is well worth attending a workshop on the subject or watching a demonstration at a textile exhibition. I think of it particularly as an item in my "design tool box". It enables me to interpret my design better.

There are a number of fabric coloring substances and they are available from specialist shops who supply arts and crafts materials. It is always advisable to make test pieces and wash them thoroughly, particularly if you will need to wash the finished article.

It is important, because you are dealing with chemicals, that you should always protect your skin and eyes and take care not to inhale any fumes.

Transfer Printing

This is a good method for anyone who feels reluctant to design straight onto the fabric because there is an intermediate stage, on paper. The design can be created using transfer crayons and transfer paints directly onto paper or from a computer print-out onto transfer paper (see below). Note that the result will be a mirror image of your design. When you are happy with the design, transfer it to your fabric by placing it face down on the fabric and ironing it with the iron as hot as the fabric will bear – test first.

Paper: Use office style paper, tracing paper or greaseproof paper. Tissue is not suitable as it's too soft.

Fabrics: The printing happens as the result of a chemical reaction, so you need to choose your fabrics carefully. It is often difficult to be sure what is a natural fiber and what is man-made, but you must choose man-made fabrics, such as nylon, for this method.

Make some trial pieces on scraps of the fabric you would like to use. I have had very good results using synthetic satins and velours. Many of the other coloring methods work best on natural fibers, so this is a useful method to know about.

Transfer Crayons: These look like children's wax crayons. They are soft and easy to use and clean to work with. Use them:
◆ to give texture to a fabric by making a rubbing from a surface, such as a piece of wood, a carving or a brick;
◆ for traced repeat motifs;
◆ for writing: write what you need the lettering to say in the size you wish in pencil on tracing paper. Then turn the paper over and color over the letters with the transfer crayons. Position the paper so that you can read the writing before you iron it onto the fabric.

Transfer Paints: These come in small plastic bottles and are ready-mixed but you can also blend the colors. Use copy paper, drawing out your design with a pencil first, if that helps. Allow the painting to dry before ironing it off. Use them :
◆ to blend a shaded mix of colors;
◆ to produce a watercolor style painting to use as a background;
◆ for repeated motifs by re-painting the design after using it a few times.

Transfer Paper: This special paper can be used in conjunction with a color ink jet printer to transfer an image created on the computer to fabric, once again by ironing.

Paper Bag Printing

This is a form of transfer printing. The ink and the pattern come from a certain kind of printed paper bag (see page 176). These bags are a byproduct of the textile printing industry and are made from paper used as a trial run for textile designs. Because the paper does not absorb the ink as well as the fabric, it can be released with the help of a hot iron. Again, test first. The heat of the iron also sets the color.

Block Printing

The paints to use for this method are quite varied and it is worth trying out what you have already, such as acrylics, as well as inquiring at your local arts and crafts shop about what will work. Experiment and wash the finished product before you commit yourself to a lot of time or money.

Blocks can be purchased or you can make your own. You may be lucky enough to find a beautifully carved old textile printing block.

To experiment with your paints and fabric, try cutting designs in polystyrene packaging, a household sponge or a potato, or use textured surfaces, such as string wrapped around a small piece of wood, the end of a cotton reel or a piece of lace.

STENCILLING

You can use ready-cut stencils or buy waxed stencil sheets to make your own.

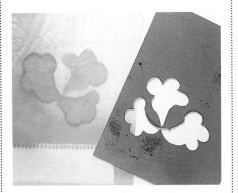

Once again, you need to experiment. Try the paints you have available. The paint needs to be fairly thick so that it does not run underneath the stencil, and there are some thickeners available. Your local craft shop will advise you. Experiment, too, with the means that you apply the paint – try a firm sponge, make a small firmer pad from a block of wood covered with a little batting and fabric, or use a stencil brush.

FABRIC MANIPULATION
Gathering

The word gathering describes the way that fabric is drawn up in puckers by pulling up a thread that has been used to make running stitches. Gathering has been used by quiltmakers for generations and perhaps the best example is the Yo-Yo, described on pages 154 to 157.

Hem a narrow strip of fabric. Run a gathering thread down the center and pull it up to make a frill, or use a machine zig-zag instead of the usual running stitch as the gathering thread.

An alternative way is a method I have called "scrunch", which I have used in the Gingham Quilt (see page 77). Work as follows:

1   Cut a square of fabric to the size required, then cut another four times as large.

2   Gather all around the edges of the larger piece and pull it up to fit the smaller one.

3   Place it on top of the smaller one and baste the edges of the two pieces of fabric together.

4   Compress the excess fabric so that it lies in irregular folds. Use small stitches to secure it.

Slashing

Sometimes you will find a whole quilt made by layering fabric and stitching lines across it before cutting between the lines on the upper fabric(s). One variation is the corduroy technique, made by slashing parallel lines. The brushed raw edges produce different effects according to whether the cuts are with the grain or on the bias. Try the following example that I have used in the Gingham Quilt.

1   Cut six 7in/17.5cm squares of the same fabric and pin together.

2   Leave a border of 1in/2.5cm all around, then stitch the square with a grid of twenty-five 1in/2.5cm squares.

3   Using a sharp craft knife or pointed scissors, cut a diagonal cross in alternate squares through all but the bottom layer. Brush up the raw edges.

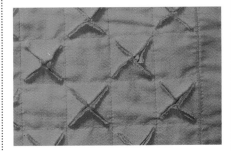

Tucks and Pleats

There are many kinds of tucks and pleats used in dressmaking and soft furnishings that can be used to create texture on a quilt. Try machining a series of regular tucks all in the same direction, then place hand stitches at intervals to pull the crests of the tucks in different directions for a regular or random pattern.

Piping

The process involves covering a filler cord with fabric, which can be on the straight grain or bias, and stitching close to the cord with the help of a zipper foot. The fabric covering is usually a separate strip that is then inserted into a seam as a strengthener. Piping is often used in this way at the edge of a quilt.

To use it as a decorative feature within the quilt top:
◆ place in the seam between the main blocks of a quilt and the border;
◆ allow extra length of fabric for covering the cord and do not stitch too close to the cord, then pull up the cord to give a ruched effect;
◆ the fabric covering the cord does not need to be a single strip – it can be a piece of patchwork itself;
◆ stitch lengths of cord into the tucks of a square, as in the Gingham Quilt (see page 77).

Rouleaux Strips
Rouleaux strips are tubes of fabric with the raw edges enclosed. They have great possibilities in terms of fabric manipulation, being softer than piping, as they have no filler cord.

1   Cut strips of fabric 1¼in/3.5cm wide on the straight of the grain.

2   Securely stitch a piece of string, longer than the strip, to the center of one end (diagram 1).

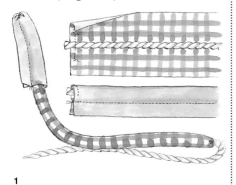

1

3   Fold the strip in two lengthways, right sides together, so that it encloses the string. Taking a ¼in/0.75cm seam and using the zipper foot, stitch along the length. Avoid stitching too close to the string.

4   Use the string to help you turn the tube right way out by pulling it through. Cut off the string and discard.

Use such rouleaux strips to make loops to set into seams or for weaving, knotting – even knitting! The center block of the Gingham Quilt consists of woven rouleaux strips.

Cathedral Window and Folded Star Patchwork
Both these methods use techniques of fabric manipulation to create their classic effects (see pages 148 and 158).

MACHINE EMBROIDERY
Needlewomen have been embellishing their quilts with embroidery for centuries. To add to hand embroidery in all its forms, we now have machine embroidery.

I like to change the appearance and surface of fabric by using the stitches on my sewing machine. Even if yours will only stitch with a straight stitch, there are still several different ways that you can use it for embroidery:
◆ use a shiny thread through the needle;
◆ use a variegated thread through the needle;
◆ use two contrasting threads through the needle at the same time;
◆ change the length of the stitch;
◆ stitch rows close together;
◆ stitch a pattern of rows;
◆ stitch on rows of braid and ribbon;
◆ stitch on strips of fabric cut with pinking shears or torn;
◆ disengage the feed dogs and stitch freely;
◆ use the technique called cable or bobbin work, where you wind a thicker thread, or one of variable thickness, onto the bobbin (underneath). You will probably need to loosen the bobbin tension.

If your machine has a zig-zag you can do all the things listed above with a zig-zag stitch as well as couching down interesting yarns and covering the edges of applied fabrics with satin stitch. Also, you will probably be able to use a twin or triple needle, which gives parallel stitching.

Many machines now have a large variety of automatic stitches – try them out to see what effect they give with different threads. Also experiment to see what they look like when you make them as large, as small and as wide or as narrow as possible.

As machines are intended for dressmaking, when you are usually stitching together two layers of fabric, you may find that your machine does not give a good result on one layer – puckering the surface. One way to counter this is by using an embroidery hoop and I like the flat plastic ones with a metal spring – these can be moved along as you work, without taking the work from under the machine – but I prefer to work with paper underneath the fabric. This can be tissue, greaseproof, "stitch and tear" or typing paper but I sometimes use freezer paper, ironing it onto the fabric before I start.

Whatever your repertoire, keep a spare piece of the fabric you are using to test out each new effect before you stitch into the actual piece.

I have used many of these variations in the Gingham Quilt (see page 77). I stitched onto a width of fabric, then cut this newly created fabric into squares to use for the patchwork.

Gingham Quilt

THIS QUILTED THROW USES THE TECHNIQUES OF FABRIC MANIPULATION AND MACHINE EMBROIDERY TO ILLUSTRATE THE EARLIER SECTION. THE NINE SELF-COLORED SQUARES WHICH FORM A FOCUS ARE WORKED SEPARATELY BUT THE STRIPED SQUARES ARE WORKED SIX AT A TIME — ACROSS THE FULL WIDTH OF THE FABRIC. YOU MAY NOT BE ABLE TO REPRODUCE THE MACHINE EMBROIDERY EXACTLY BUT, USING THE IDEAS LISTED, YOU'LL BE ABLE TO PRODUCE A SIMILAR RESULT, INDIVIDUAL TO YOU.

Quilt size: 42in/107cm square

Materials

- ⊡ Top and backing: 5½yards/5m of 45in/115cm wide plain cotton fabric — mine is a pale red
- ⊡ Strongly contrasting machine thread — mine is cream
- ⊡ Matching machine thread
- ⊡ Pearl cotton in each of the two colors
- ⊡ 5½yards/5m of 4 or 5 fancy knitting yarns in each of the two colors
- ⊡ Piping cord, 5mm thick
- ⊡ Batting: 2oz, 45in/114cm square
- ⊡ 36 small buttons for the ties

CUTTING

1 For each of the four scrunch squares, cut one square of fabric 7in/17.5cm square and one 13in/33cm square.

2 For each of the four squares with frayed crosses, cut six squares of fabric 7in/17.5cm square.

3 For the central square, cut one piece of fabric 7in/17.5cm square and four strips across the width, each measuring 1½in/4cm.

4 For the sixteen squares with cream lines, cut three strips across the width, each measuring 7in/17.5cm.

5 For the twenty-four self-colored squares, cut four strips across the width, each measuring 9in/23cm.

6 For the backing, cut one square, 45 x 45in/114 x 114cm.

EMBROIDERY AND FABRIC MANIPULATION SQUARES

Be adventurous in your stitching – but remember to try out each method first.

1 Using your sewing machine to its full capacity and the contrast threads, follow the ideas given in the section on embroidery (see page 75) to embroider long rows of decoration on the three strips of 7in/17.5cm wide fabric. Aim to have a good variety.

2 With the matching threads, work on the four 9in/23cm strips. Use the extra width to create tucks and pleats. Stitch rows of piping into tucks and stitch on additional gathered frills. Be careful not make the strip measure less than 7in/17.5cm wide and if it is more than this when completed, trim it to measure 7in/17.5cm before moving to the next stage.

3 When the strips are embellished, iron them from the reverse side. Cut the contrast embroidered strips into sixteen 7in/17.5cm squares. Cut the self-colored, manipulated strips into twenty-four 7in/17.5cm squares.

FEATURE SQUARES

Refer to the sections on gathering, slashing and rouleaux strips on pages 74 to 75.

1 Make four "scrunch" squares and four squares with frayed crosses.

2 For the central square, use the four 1½in/4cm strips to make rouleaux, then cut into twenty-four 7in/17.5cm lengths. Stitch twelve of these to the top and bottom of the plain square close together to form the warp. Use the rest as the weft to weave a plain weave pattern (under one, over one), then stitch down the ends (diagram 1).

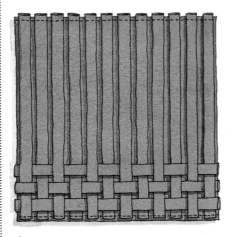

1

ASSEMBLING THE PATCHWORK

1 Taking a ½in/1.5cm seam, join the squares together as shown in the quilt assembly diagram. Make seven rows of seven squares first, then join the rows together.

2 Press the seams so that the cut rows of stitching lie over the adjacent patches (diagram 2).

2

FINISHING

1 Lay out the quilt, right side up. cover this with the backing fabric, right side down, and cover this with batting, smoothing out each layer to prevent wrinkles.

2 Use safety pins, with at least one in each square, around the edge of the sandwich, to hold the layers together.

3 Taking a ½in/1.5cm seam and working with the quilt top uppermost, stitch around the edges of the quilt, leaving a 9in/23cm gap in one side.

4 Trim off any excess batting and backing from the seam and clip all the layers at the corners. Turn the quilt through to the right side through the gap. Pull out the corners, so that they are sharp right angles, then slipstitch the gap to close.

5 Stitch on the buttons through all the layers at the junctions of the squares as shown in the quilt assembly plan. You might like to use the pearl thread for this and leave long ends on the knots on the reverse of the quilt.

SPEED PIECING

ROTARY CUTTING

Rotary cutting has transformed the way traditional patchwork is done, making it possible to cut quickly and accurately. And because it saves so much time on the routine work of cutting shapes, it allows more for the labour-intensive details, such as quilting.

EQUIPMENT

Equipment required includes: self-healing mat, rotary cutter, plastic rulers in a variety of sizes (see pages 8 and 10).

I would suggest you buy a mat at least 24in/60cm in length, so that you can cut the width of most cotton fabrics folded selvage to selvage. A medium cutter is most practical, but for appliqué work, a small cutter is also useful. Try to keep a spare blade, as these do eventually blunt (though they can be sharpened). Save old blades for cutting paper and craft projects. Recommended sizes of ruler for strip piecing are 24in and 6in. A 9½in square ruler is also very helpful.

Tip *Stick small dots of sandpaper on the underside of the ruler to help it grip the fabric as you cut. It is much less frustrating and safer as well, especially for cutting long strips.*

CUTTING STRIPS

One of the most useful techniques using the rotary cutter is to cut strips for strip-pieced blocks (see page 84) or for borders. Work with the whole width of the fabric.

Trimming the fabric

1 Fold the fabric in half from selvage to selvage. Make sure that it lies flat. The ends may be slightly askew.

2 It is important to trim the ends evenly, before beginning to cut strips. Place the fold of the fabric near the bottom edge of the mat.

3 Position the ruler so that its long edge is close to the raw edges of the fabric and one of the short horizontal lines lies exactly on the fold. You may need to move the ruler further to the left in order to expose both the raw edges of the fabric (diagram 1).

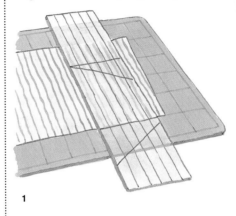

1

4 Hold the ruler down firmly with one hand and place the rotary cutter at the fold of the fabric abutting the ruler with the other. Open the blade and cut **away from your body** down the length of the ruler to the selvages.

Note *Always cut away from your body. Rotary cutters are very sharp and care must be taken when using this wonderful tool.*

5 Immediately retract the blade, then remove the rough edge of the fabric. You now have a clean exact edge to begin cutting strips.

Cutting

You must know the exact finished size of strip required before cutting, then add ¼in/0.75cm seam allowances on either side. For example, for a finished width of 1in/2.5cm, cut the strips 1½in/4cm wide.

1 Turn the fabric, so that the trimmed edge is on the left and the fold still at the bottom. Carefully place the ruler over the fabric, so that the

appropriate vertical measurement on the ruler is exactly aligned with the trimmed edge of the fabric. Cut as before (diagram 2).

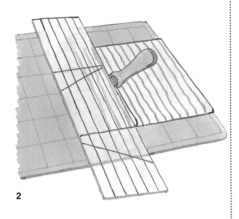

2

2 Open up the strip. It should be evenly cut along its length. If it has a slight "V" shape, you need to re-trim the edge of the folded fabric.

Cutting Smaller Strips

Having cut long strips across the width of the fabric (normally approximately 45in/115cm), you may need to cut smaller lengths.

1 Trim off the selvages, then place the strip across the mat – following a straight line on the mat may help.

2 Align the ruler as before and cut the length required (diagram 3).

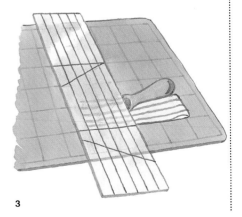

3

SUB-CUTTING STRIPS TO MAKE OTHER SHAPES

Strips can be cut to create different geometrical shapes without using templates. This is called sub-cutting.

Sub-cutting Squares

1   First determine the size of square needed, adding the usual seam allowances, e.g. for a 3in/7.5cm finished square, work to a 3½in/9cm measurement. Cut a strip 3½in/9cm wide as above, then place the strip lengthwise across the mat.

2   Place the ruler with the vertical line aligned at 3½in/9cm and the horizontal line aligned with the edge of the strip (diagram 4). Cut along the side of the ruler to get a 3½in/9cm square. Repeat down the width of the strip until you have cut the required number of squares.

Sub-cutting Half-square Triangles

1   For half-square triangles, first cut the squares to the finished size plus ⅞in/2.25cm, e.g. 6⅞in/17.25cm, as described above.

2   Align the edge of the ruler diagonally across the square from corner to corner and cut. You now have two half-square triangles (diagram 5) which, when joined to other half square triangles and sewn into the quilt, will give two bi-colored 6in/15cm squares.

Sub-cutting Quarter-square Triangles

1   These can be cut by adding 1¼in/3cm to the finished size of square required, e.g. for a 6in/15cm finished square, cut squares 7¼in/18cm.

2   Cut across the diagonal of these squares in both directions and you will have four quarter-square triangles (diagram 6).

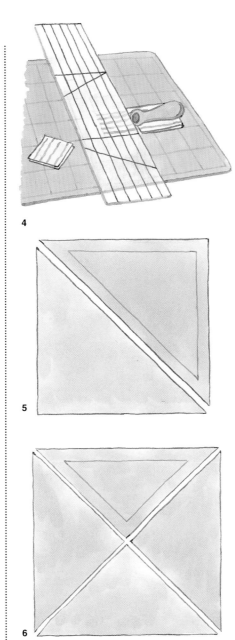

4

5

6

7

Sub-cutting Half Rectangles

1   Add 1¼in/3cm to the finished length measurement and ⅝in/1.5cm to the finished width measurement, then cut a strip to the width required.

2   Cut across the strip to the length required, then sub-cut across the diagonal of the rectangle (diagram 7).

CHAIN PIECING

Chain piecing is an excellent way to save thread and save time.

1   Place two pieces right sides together and sew along the seam line.

2   Do not clip the threads or remove the pieces from the machine, but, with the needle raised, gently pull them towards the back of the machine and feed in another two pieces of fabric (again right sides together) and sew along the seam line (diagram 8). Continue in this way without cutting the threads in between the pieces.

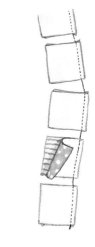

8

3   When you have the requisite number of pieces, clip the threads and remove from the machine. Clip the threads between the pieces and press the pieces open.

Rail Fence

RAIL FENCE IS A SIMPLE DESIGN TO CONSTRUCT USING QUICK CUTTING AND PIECING TECHNIQUES AND HAS GREAT POSSIBILITIES FOR DRAMA IN CHOICE AND PLACEMENT OF FABRIC. IT IS MADE UP ESSENTIALLY OF BLOCKS MADE FROM JOINED STRIPS, PLACED ALTERNATELY HORIZONTALLY AND VERTICALLY. THE STRIP WIDTHS I'VE CHOSEN CREATE A BASKET-WEAVE EFFECT. THIS QUILT IS MADE FROM FLANNEL, A FAIRLY HEAVY, BRUSHED COTTON AVAILABLE IN A SELECTION OF PATTERNED AND PLAIN FABRICS. I USED A WOOL BATTING WHICH MAKES A LOVELY SOFT LAP QUILT FOR COLD WINTER EVENINGS.

Quilt size: 57 x 64in/145 x 163cm

Materials

All fabrics used in the quilt top are 40in/100cm wide
- ▣ Rotary cutter, ruler and mat
- ▣ Fabric A: 1¼yards/1.25m, pink flannel
- ▣ Fabric B: 1½yards/1.5m, dark pink patterned flannel
- ▣ Inner border: ½yard/50cm

- ▣ Middle border and binding: 1yard/1m
- ▣ Outer border: 1¼yards/1.25m
- ▣ Backing: 65 x 72in/165 x 183cm
- ▣ Batting: wool, 61 x 68in/155 x 173cm

CUTTING

1   For the blocks, from fabric A, cut twenty-four 1¼in/4cm strips and from fabric B, sixteen 3in/7.5cm strips across the width of the fabric.

2   From the inner border fabric, cut six 2in/5cm strips.

3   From the middle border fabric, cut six 1¼in/3cm strips.

4   From the outer border fabric cut six 6½in/16.5cm strips, all across the width of the fabric.

5   For the binding, cut seven 2in/5cm strips from the middle border fabric, across the width of the fabric.

STITCHING

1   Taking a ¼in/0.75cm seam allowance, stitch one strip of fabric A to one of fabric B to make a strip AB. Repeat to make sixteen pairs.

2   Press the seam allowances together towards the darker strip.

3   Join the two AB strips together, taking the usual seam allowance.

4   Add a third strip of fabric A to fabric B on the joined strip to make the sequence, ABABA (diagram 1). Press the seam allowances as above.

5   Make up seven more ABABA strips in this way.

6   Sub-cut each set of strips into 8½in/21.5cm squares (diagram 2). You will get at least four from each set of strips and you need a total of 30 squares.

ASSEMBLING

1   Following the quilt assembly plan, lay out the squares in six rows of five, alternating horizontal and vertically placed squares.

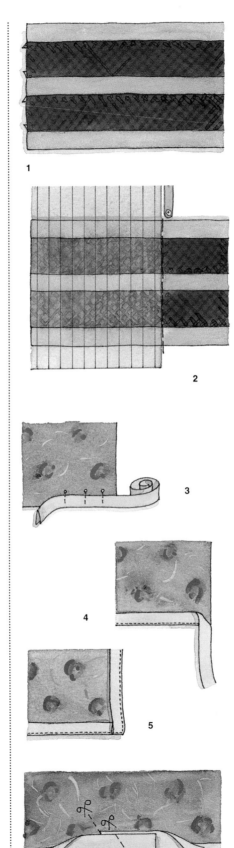

2   Stitch the first row of blocks together, taking a ¼in/0.75cm seam allowance. Press the seams all in one direction.

3   Stitch the second row of blocks together and press the seams in the opposite direction. Continue to stitch the remaining rows together, alternating the direction of the seams.

4   Stitch the rows together. Because you have pressed the seams in alternate directions, you will be able to butt the seams together. Press the seams towards the bottom of the quilt.

ADDING THE BORDERS

1   Determine the length of the two inner side borders by measuring from top edge to bottom edge through the center. Trim two of the cut strips to this measurement, joining the strips if necessary to make the required length.

2   Pin and stitch the borders to the quilt sides. Press the seams towards the borders.

3   Determine the length of the top and bottom borders by measuring from side edge to side edge through the center. Trim two of the cut strips to this measurement, joining as necessary.

4   Pin and stitch the borders to the top and bottom edges of the quilt and press the seams towards the borders.

5   For the middle border, repeat steps 1 to 4, trimming the cut strips to the required measurements.

6   For the outer border, repeat steps 1 to 4, trimming the cut strips to the required measurements. The quilt top is now complete.

FINISHING

1   Lay out the backing, right side down, smoothing out any wrinkles, and center the batting on top. Center the pieced top over the batting, right side up.

2   Sew lines of basting about 4in/11cm apart across the quilt from top to bottom and side to side, through all three layers.

3   Quilt by hand or machine as you prefer. I machined "in-the-ditch", then across on the diagonal from quilt block to quilt block. This enables the quilt to be secure without detracting from the woven look. The borders are outlined "in-the-ditch" and the outer border is stippled in a meandering curvy line to secure the three layers.

4   For the binding, cut and join enough strips, 2in/5cm wide, from the middle border fabric to make a total length of 255in/637cm. Fold in half lengthwise and roll up into a coil.

5   Trim the edges of the batting and backing level with the pieced top, then pin the folded (and coiled) binding on the bottom edge of the quilt sandwich, leaving about 12in/30cm free (diagram 3).

6   Sew the binding to the quilt sandwich, taking a ¼in/0.75cm seam, to within ¼in/0.75cm of the corner. Fold the binding down and away from the quilt top (diagram 4), then back on itself up the next side of the quilt. Start stitching again and continue to ¼in/0.75cm before the next corner (diagram 5).

7   Repeat as for the first corner and continue around the quilt until you are about 18in/45cm from where you started. Open out the binding and place the starting tail just inside it. Mark a 45 degree angle along the line of the join and measure ½in/1.5cm from this marking on the ending tail towards the direction of the start. Cut along this line (diagram 6). Take the two loose ends of the beginning and ending, open them and sew together with a ¼in/0.75cm seam allowance. Finger press to one side. Then fold over and continue to sew the joined binding to the quilt top until you reach the start.

8   To finish the binding, fold over to the back of the quilt and stitch down, covering the previous line of stitching.

Devil's Puzzle

THIS IS THE FIRST OF SIX CLASSIC QUILTS USING TECHNIQUES EXPLAINED EARLIER IN THE BOOK. IT IS A VARIATION ON THE CLASSIC "DRUNKARD'S PATH" PATTERN AND WAS A GREAT FAVORITE AMONG THE EARLY AMERICAN PIONEERS. MANY ANTIQUE QUILTS IN THIS PATTERN HAVE SURVIVED. ONCE YOU HAVE MASTERED THE CURVED SEAM, THE QUILT IS VERY EASILY PUT TOGETHER. IT HAS BEEN MACHINE-STITCHED BUT CAN EQUALLY WELL BE PIECED BY HAND. I HAVE USED A GREAT NUMBER OF SCRAPS IN THIS QUILT TO GIVE IT AN "ANTIQUE" FEEL. THIS SIZE IS SUITABLE FOR A DOUBLE BED COVER.

Quilt size: 78 x 86in/198 x 218cm

Materials

All fabrics used in the quilt top are 45in/115cm wide

☑ Binding: ½yard/45cm, plain cotton to coordinate with patterns

☑ Print fabrics: 2½yards/2.30m total of a good selection of print cottons for a scrap quilt effect

☑ Plain fabric: 2½yards/2.30m muslin

☑ Backing: 84 x 92in/213 x 233cm, plain cotton

☑ Batting: 2oz, 84 x 92in/213 x 233cm

CUTTING

1 Cut six strips 2½in /7cm wide for the binding.

2 Trace templates A and B from page 89 and cut out in cardboard or template plastic without seam allowance.

3 On the wrong side of the fabric, accurately draw around templates A and B and cut out adding a ¼in/0.75cm seam allowance. You will use this pencil line as your stitching guide. For each block, cut 20 A pieces from print scraps and 16 A pieces from muslin, plus 16 B pieces from scraps and 20 B pieces from muslin. For each partial block, cut 8 A pieces from scraps, 4 A pieces from muslin, 4 B pieces from scraps and 8 B pieces from muslin.

STITCHING

Each block is made up of 36 smaller squares, which in turn are made up from one piece A and one B, one from scrap and one from muslin, joined with a curved seam. You will need to make nine blocks, six partial blocks and 44 individual smaller squares.

1 To piece a curved seam work as follows: place scrap piece B on the work surface, right side up, and lay muslin piece A, right side down, on top.

2 Pin the righthand corner, aligning raw edges, then pin the left hand corner aligning raw edges. Gently fit the curved edge of A to the curve of B and pin with pins perpendicular to the edge, clipping into the seam allowance of piece A (diagram 1).

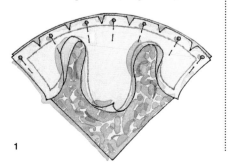

1

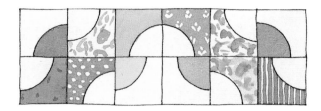

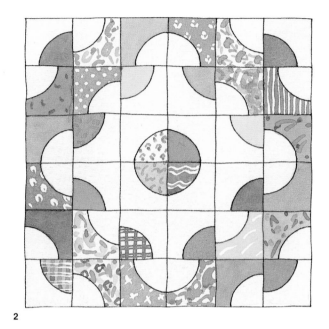

2

3 Machine stitch the seam. The pins can be left in until you reach the end of the seam.

4 Repeat to join all the pieces A and B into small squares, always joining a scrap fabric piece to a muslin piece.

5 Referring to the block diagrams (diagram 2), sew the finished squares into strips, arranging the colored pieces in a pleasing design but keeping the muslin pieces as shown.

6 Sew the strips together into a block. Make a total of nine blocks and six partial blocks.

7 Press all the curved seams away from the muslin and all the straight seams to one side.

8 Following the quilt assembly plan on page 86, join the partial blocks into two rows, then the full blocks into three rows. Add the extra small squares into units at the ends of each row. Finally, join the rows, carefully matching and pinning seams.

FINISHING

1 Lay out the backing, right side down, smoothing out any wrinkles, and center the batting on top.

2 Center the pieced top, right side up, over the batting and sew lines of basting about 4in/11cm apart across the quilt from top to bottom and side to side through all three layers.

3 Quilt by hand or machine about ¼in/0.75cm in from the edge on the muslin following the block design.

4 When all the quilting has been completed, bind with a double-fold binding (see page 23).

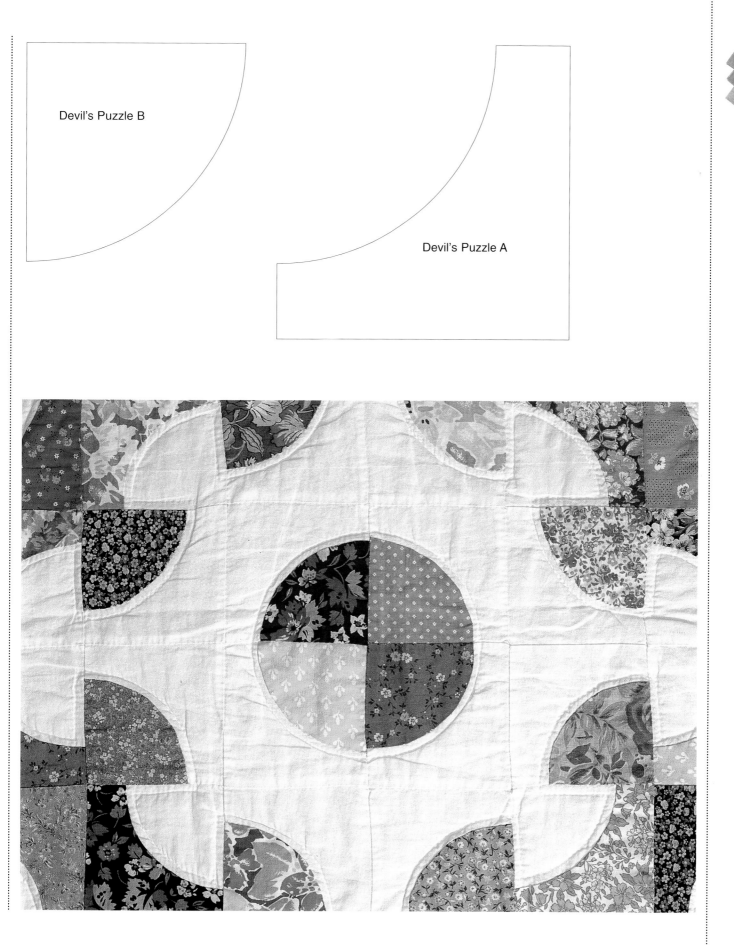

Devil's Puzzle B

Devil's Puzzle A

Sugar Mountain

THE SECOND CLASSIC QUILT USES A TRADITIONAL BLOCK KNOWN AS "SUGAR LOAF". IT ORIGINATES FROM THE DAYS WHEN SUGAR, SO OFTEN IN SHORT SUPPLY, WAS TIGHTLY PACKED INTO A CONE-SHAPED WRAPPING OF BLUE PAPER. IN MY QUILT, "SUGAR MOUNTAIN", I HAVE USED A WIDE VARIETY OF COLORED AND PATTERNED COTTON FABRICS, OFFSET AGAINST A PLAIN BLUE BACKGROUND. THE DESIGN CAN BE JUST AS EYE-CATCHING USING A MORE LIMITED CHOICE OF COLORS. THE KEY TO A PLEASING VISUAL MIX IN THIS DESIGN IS THE SKILLFUL USE OF LIGHT, MEDIUM AND DARK TONES WITHIN A SELECTION OF COLORS.

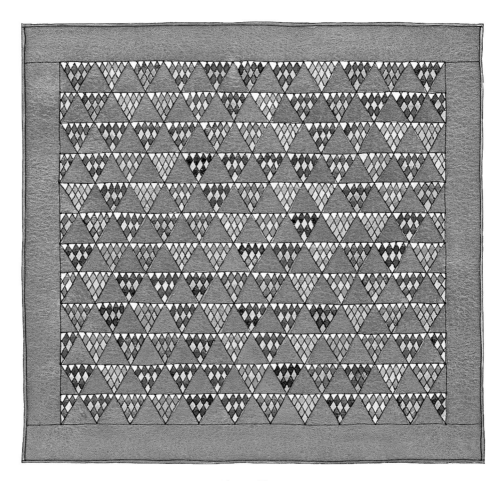

Quilt size: 70½ x 73½in/179 x 186cm

Materials

All fabrics used in the quilt top are 45in/115cm wide

- ▣ Patterned dark tone fabrics: 140 strips of assorted colors 1½ x 18in/4 x 45.5cm
- ▣ 12 x 18in rotary cutting ruler with 60° marking line
- ▣ Patterned medium tone fabrics: 140 strips of assorted colors 1½ x15in/4 x 38cm

- ▣ Light fabric: 2¼yards/2m
- ▣ Background fabric, borders and binding: 5¾yards/5.25m blue cotton
- ▣ Backing: 4½yards/4.25m blue cotton
- ▣ Batting: 76 x 79in/193 x 201cm

CUTTING

1 From the dark strips, using the rotary cutting ruler to line the 60° mark up against the long edge of the fabric strips, rotary cut at 1½in/4cm intervals, creating 60° diamonds from each strip (diagram 1). You should get six per strip, totalling 840.

2 From the medium strips, cut four 60° diamonds from each strip as before, to a total of 560 diamonds.

Tip *Keep the diamonds in separate containers pinned together in sets of four medium tone fabrics and six dark tones.*

3 Cut the light fabric into 1¾in/4.5cm strips, then sub-cut as before at 1¾in/4.5cm intervals, into 60° diamonds, to a total of 350. Cut the diamonds in half to create two equilateral triangles (five per block = 700 triangles).

4 From the background fabric, cut four strips for the borders, 6½in/16.5cm wide and approximately 100in/254cm long. They will be cut to size at a later stage.

5 Also from the background fabric, cut 5¼in/14.75cm strips and sub-cut as before at 5¼in/14.75cm intervals to create 60° diamonds, to a total of 63. Cut each diamond in half to create two equilateral triangles (126 in total).

6 For the half triangles at the row ends, cut a strip from the background fabric, 6¼in/16cm wide and 40in/1 metre long. Sub-cut at 6¼in/16cm intervals to create diamonds; cut in half crosswise to create triangles, then cut the triangles in half again lengthwise (12 half triangles required for 6 rows).

7 From the background fabric, cut strips on the bias, 1½in/4cm wide, to a total length of 293in/744cm.

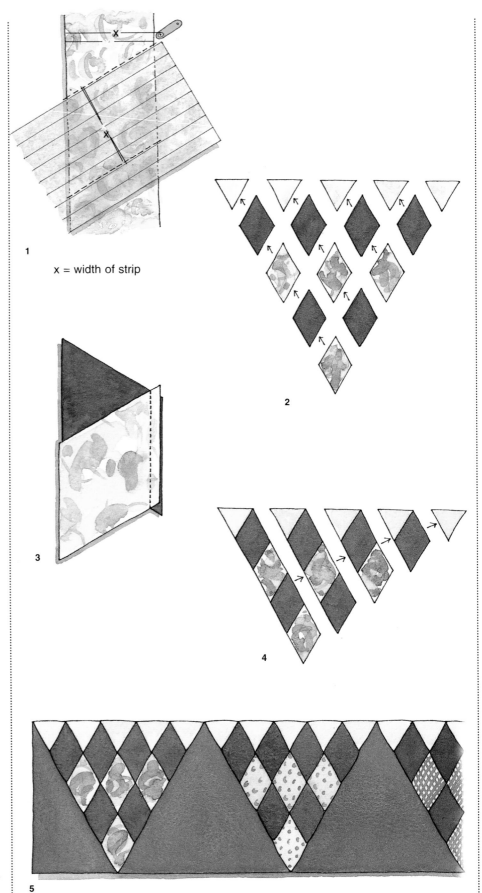

1

x = width of strip

2

3

4

5

STITCHING

1 From the fabric containers, select a set of six dark diamonds, a set of four medium diamonds and five light triangles. Stitch together in rows (diagram 2), being careful to offset the seam allowance (diagram 3).

Tip *It is helpful to have the straight of grain of the light triangles along the outer edge of the block, to help hold the block to size when piecing the completed rows.*

2 Press the seams of the first row in one direction and the seams of second row in the opposite direction and so on, to enable a "good meet" where seams join and distribute bulk.

3 Stitch the rows together to form a pieced triangle (diagram 4).

4 Stitch the pieced triangles together with plain background triangles, with a plain half triangle at each end to create the first row of the quilt top (diagram 5).

5 To create the second row, stitch fully pieced triangles at each end, then trim, but add the seam allowance before cutting. Discard the cut-off pieces.

6 Following the quilt assembly plan, stitch a total of twelve rows, then stitch the rows together.

ADDING THE BORDERS

1 Determine the length of the two side borders by measuring the quilt top from top edge to bottom edge through the center. Trim two of the border strips to this measurement.

2 Stitch the borders to the sides. Press the seams towards the borders.

3 Determine the length of the top and bottom borders by measuring the quilt top from side edge to side edge through the center. Trim the remaining two border strips to this measurement.

4 Stitch the borders to the top and bottom edges of the quilt and press the seams towards the borders.

Note *In the quilt photographed on page 91, I have incorporated extra triangle blocks into the borders as a finishing touch to add visual effect.*

FINISHING

1 Cut the backing fabric in half crosswise and join. Trim to measure 76 x 79in/193 x 201cm. Press.

2 Lay out the backing, right side down, smoothing out any wrinkles, and center the batting on top.

3 Center the pieced top, right side up, over the batting, then sew lines of basting about 4in/11cm apart across the quilt from top to bottom and side to side through all three layers.

4 Quilt by hand. I have stitched a cross hatch design throughout the pieced area, with the lines running through the center of the diamonds. A rope twist design has been stitched in the borders.

5 Join the binding strips and use to bind the quilt with a double-fold binding (see page 85).

Double Wedding Ring

THIS THIRD TRADITIONAL PATTERN WAS VERY POPULAR IN THE 1930S. IT'S IDEAL FOR USING UP EVEN THE TINIEST SCRAPS, BUT IF A PLANNED ARRANGEMENT OF FABRICS IS USED, SECONDARY PATTERNS CAN APPEAR. IT IS A CHALLENGING DESIGN FOR AN EXPERIENCED QUILTER BECAUSE OF THE NEED FOR ACCURATE PIECING USING CURVED SEAMS. THE CENTRAL AREAS GIVE SCOPE FOR DETAILED QUILTING. IT CAN BE MADE BY HAND OR MACHINE. IF YOU INTEND TO PIECE BY HAND, DRAW AROUND THE TEMPLATES ACCURATELY AND USE THIS AS THE STITCHING LINE. ADD SEAM ALLOWANCES BY EYE WHEN YOU CUT OUT AND PIN CAREFULLY.

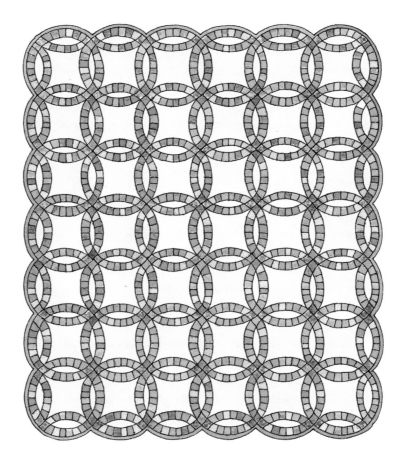

Quilt size: 80 x 90in/203 x 229cm

Materials

All the fabrics used in the quilt top are 45in/115cm wide
- ▣ Centers and melons: 5½yards/5m muslin or similar
- ▣ Arcs: 1¼yards/1m each of six fabrics (or scraps to total this amount)
- ▣ Corners: ½yard/50cm each of two fabrics (or scraps to total this amount)

- ▣ Backing: 2¾yards/2.5m, 108in/274cm wide or 5½yards/5m, 45in/115cm wide
- ▣ Batting: 84 x 94in/214 x 239cm
- ▣ Binding: 1¼yards/1m of one of the arc or corner fabrics

CUTTING

1 Trace templates A to E from page 97 and cut out in cardboard or template plastic. Note that the templates do not include seam allowances, these are added by eye when the pieces are cut. Label the templates.

2 Using templates A and B, draw around each one onto the muslin, then cut 127 melons and 56 centers, adding seam allowances by eye.

3 Using template C, cut a total of 254 arc pieces from four of the arc fabrics, adding seam allowances by eye.

4 Using template D, cut 64 arc end pieces as before from each of the remaining two arc fabrics, then reverse the template (Dr) and cut another 64 pieces from each of these two fabrics. Keep these in four separate piles.

5 Using template E, cut 128 corner pieces from each of the two corner fabrics as before.

STITCHING

1 Take the arc pieces ("C") and arrange them in your chosen order. Chain piece them together in pairs (508 sets). Press all the seams in the same direction.

2 Chain piece two sets of pairs together to make 254 arcs of four pieces each (diagram 1a).

3 Stitch the arc ends ("D" and "Dr") to each arc (diagram 1b).

4 Stitch one melon to 127 arcs, matching the center seam on the arc to the center mark on the melon edge. Pin at right angles to the seam line, match up ends and centers, then ease in between, pinning regularly to distribute any fullness evenly (diagram 1c). Note that the edges will not line up after stitching. Press seams towards the arcs.

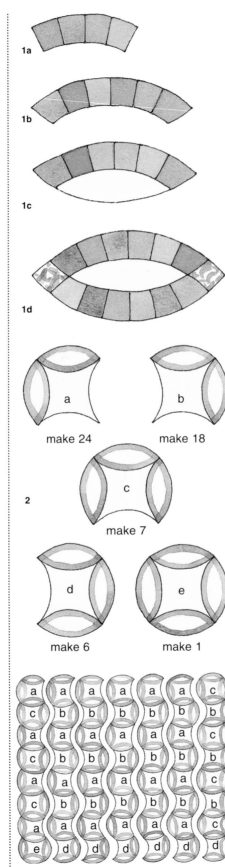

5 Take the remaining arcs and stitch a corner piece to each end, putting the same fabric on each end. You will have 63 arcs of one fabric and 64 of the other.

6 Stitch these arc sections to the opposite sides of the melons, making 127 completed units (diagram 1d). Press seams towards the arcs.

7 Following diagram 2, make 56 "clamshell" units by stitching two or more melons to each center. It is important that all corners of one color are positioned vertically and all corners of the other are positioned horizontally. Press all seams towards the arcs.

8 Following diagram 3, stitch the "clamshells" into seven vertical rows, carefully matching the points.

9 Stitch the rows together, carefully matching and pinning intersections to complete the quilt top.

FINISHING

1 Cut and stitch the backing fabric to make a piece, 84 x 94in/214 x 239cm. Lay out the backing, smoothing out any wrinkles, and center the batting on top, aligning raw edges.

2 Center the pieced top, right side up, over the batting, then sew lines of basting about 4in/11cm apart across the quilt from top to bottom and side to side through all three layers.

3 Quilt by hand or machine as desired. I have outline quilted around the rings with a motif in the centers.

4 Cut the binding fabric into 2½in/6cm wide strips, on the bias, then piece together to make a total length of at least 400in/1016cm.

5 Fold in half lengthwise, wrong sides together, and press. Line up the

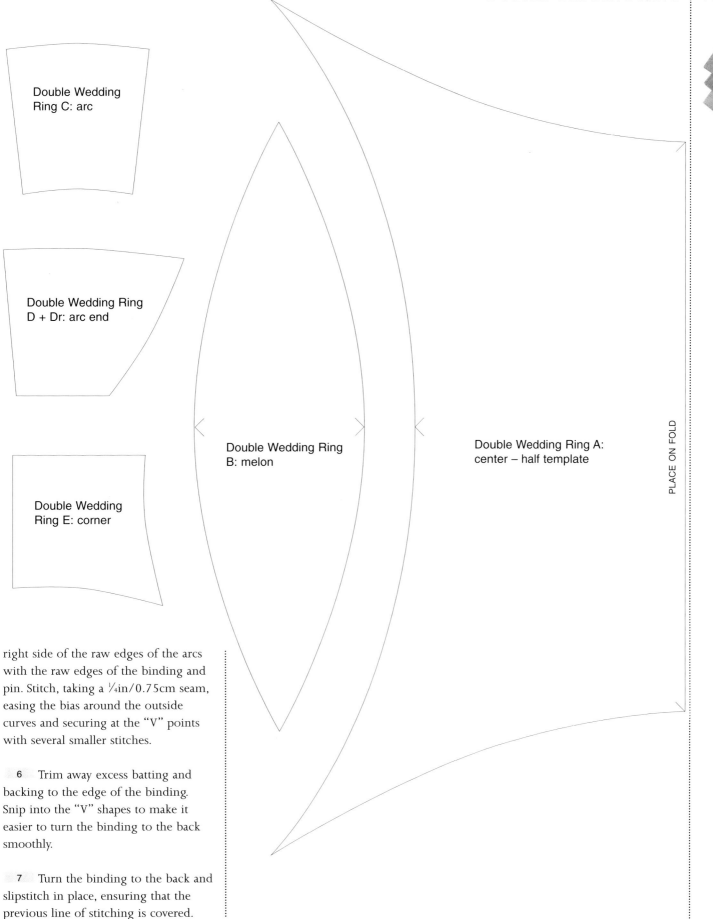

Double Wedding Ring C: arc

Double Wedding Ring D + Dr: arc end

Double Wedding Ring E: corner

Double Wedding Ring B: melon

Double Wedding Ring A: center – half template

PLACE ON FOLD

right side of the raw edges of the arcs with the raw edges of the binding and pin. Stitch, taking a ¼in/0.75cm seam, easing the bias around the outside curves and securing at the "V" points with several smaller stitches.

6   Trim away excess batting and backing to the edge of the binding. Snip into the "V" shapes to make it easier to turn the binding to the back smoothly.

7   Turn the binding to the back and slipstitch in place, ensuring that the previous line of stitching is covered.

Bear's Paw Group Quilt

THE FOURTH CLASSIC QUILT, "BEAR'S PAW", IS A GROUP SCRAP QUILT MADE BY MEMBERS OF THE QUILTING GROUP CALLED BEAR'S PAW QUILTERS. THE GROUP, BASED IN ENGLAND IN A SMALL KENT VILLAGE CALLED BURHAM, WAS FOUNDED IN 1995 BY SUSIE CORKE AND KAREN RYDER. THIS TRADITIONAL DESIGN WAS THE OBVIOUS CHOICE FOR THEIR FIRST GROUP QUILT. AT THE TIME OF MAKING, THE GROUP HAD 25 MEMBERS — A CONVENIENT NUMBER FOR A QUILT — EACH MEMBER STITCHED ONE BLOCK MAKING FIVE ROWS OF FIVE BLOCKS. THE HAND-QUILTING WAS ALSO SHARED BY THE GROUP.

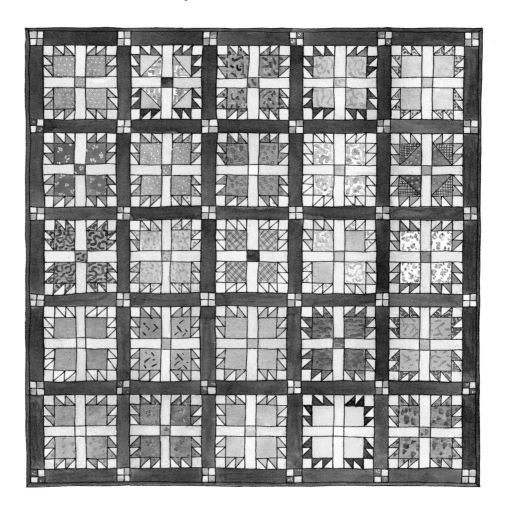

Quilt size: 64 x 64in/163 x 163cm

Materials

All fabrics used in the quilt top are 45in/115cm wide

- ▣ Blocks: 25 fat eighths of print fabrics
- ▣ Background: 25 fat eighths of cream fabrics
- ▣ Sashing: 2¼yards/2m of dark tone fabric

- ▣ Binding: 1yard/1m, same fabric as sashing
- ▣ Backing: 4yards/3.75m
- ▣ Batting: low loft, 70 x 70in/178 x 178cm
- ▣ Quilting thread in contrast color

CUTTING

1 Trace templates A to F from page 101 and cut out in cardboard or template plastic. Label the templates.

2 For each block cut:
16 template A from 1st print fabric;
16 template A from 1st cream fabric;
4 template C from 2nd print fabric;
4 template B from 2nd cream fabric;
1 template B from 3rd print fabric;
4 template D from 3rd cream fabric.

3 For the whole top cut:
60 template F from sashing fabric;
72 template E from a mix of print fabrics;
cut 72 template E from a mix of cream fabrics.

4 From the binding, cut strips on the bias, 1½in/4cm wide, to a total length of 264in/672cm.

STITCHING

1 Each block uses three print and three cream fabrics. Pin, with right sides together, and stitch, by hand or machine, sixteen pairs of one print and one cream triangle (A) to make squares.

2 Pin and stitch the squares together into eight sets of pairs, alternating directions (diagram 1a). Add a cream square (B) to the end of four sets of pairs (diagram 1b).

3 Pin and stitch one pair of triangle sets and one pair of triangle sets with added cream square to two sides of one square (C), (diagram 2). Repeat three more times.

4 Pin and stitch one sashing strip (D) between two of the sets just formed. Repeat for the bottom half of the block (diagram 3).

5 Pin and stitch one colored sashing square (B) between two sashing strips (diagram 3).

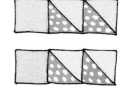
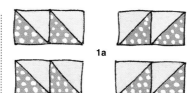
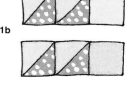

1a **1b**

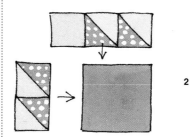

2

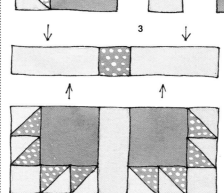

3

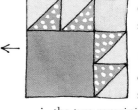

7 Pin and stitch the three pieced sections together to complete the block. Make a total of 25 blocks in this way.

8 Pin and stitch sashing squares (E) in pairs, then stitch the pairs together into a square. Make a total of 36 squares in this way.

9 Pin and stitch four vertical sashing strips between five blocks into a row. Repeat to make five rows.

10 Pin and stitch four sashing squares between five horizontal sashing strips. Repeat to make eight rows.

11 Following the quilt assembly plan, pin and stitch four horizontal sashing rows between five rows of blocks, carefully matching seams.

12 Pin and stitch a sashing strip to each side of the pieced top, carefully matching seams.

13 Pin and stitch one pieced sashing square to each end of the two remaining horizontal sashing rows, then stitch these to the top and bottom of the pieced top.

FINISHING

1 Cut the backing fabric in half crosswise and join. Trim to measure 70 x 70in/178 x 178cm. Press.

2 Lay out the backing, right side down, smoothing out any wrinkles, and center the batting on top.

3 Center the pieced top, right side up, over the batting, then sew lines of basting about 4in/11cm apart across the quilt from top to bottom and side to side through all three layers.

4 Quilt by hand using a contrasting color of quilting thread. The "Bear's Paw Group Quilt" is echo quilted in the block areas with a rope twist design in the strippy areas.

5 Join the binding strips and use to bind the quilt with a double-fold binding (see page 85).

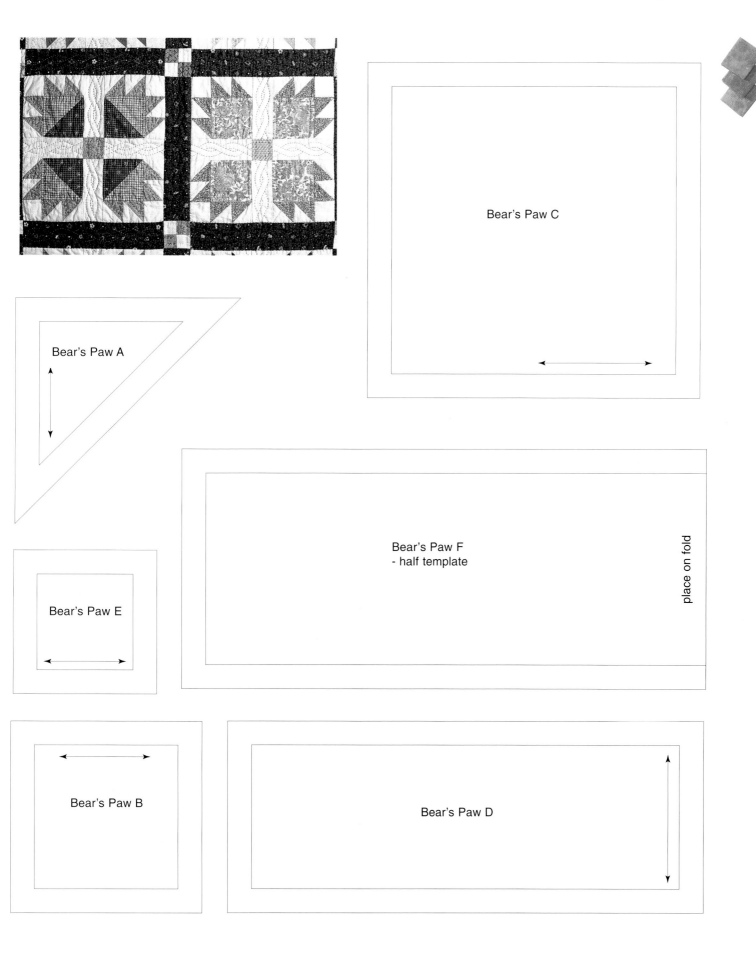

Bear's Paw C

Bear's Paw A

Bear's Paw F
- half template

place on fold

Bear's Paw E

Bear's Paw B

Bear's Paw D

Picture House Quilt

MANY TRADITIONAL QUILT BLOCKS WERE GIVEN NAMES REFERRING TO THE ENVIRONMENT AND EXPERIENCES OF THEIR MAKERS. IT IS A SHORT STEP FROM THESE TO THE REPRESENTATIONAL OR PICTURE BLOCKS WHICH SHOW, IN A MORE RECOGNISABLE WAY, ELEMENTS OF THE PIONEER LIFE. WITH A LITTLE INGENUITY, BASKETS, FLOWERS, FANS, SAILBOATS AND MANY OTHERS WERE INTERPRETED AS PIECED PATCHWORK BLOCKS. THE "SCHOOLHOUSE" QUILTS, ON WHICH THIS QUILT IS BASED, WERE OFTEN MADE AS A GIFT FOR A DEPARTING SCHOOL TEACHER. THE HOUSE QUILT REPRESENTS HEARTH AND HOME AND THIS, TEAMED WITH THE WELCOMING SOFTNESS OF A QUILT, IS AN IRRESISTIBLE COMBINATION AS A HOUSEWARMING GIFT.

Quilt size: 52 x 52in/132 x 132cm

Materials

Except where stated, all fabrics used in the quilt top are 45in/115cm wide

▣ Each block needs seven or eight fabrics in the following sizes: House walls: 9 x 12in/23 x 30cm

    Roof/chimney: 9 x 12in/23 x 30cm

    Door, windows and ground: scraps of three or four fabrics, including two harmonizing light colors for windows

    Background: 1½in/4cm wide strips to a total length of 55in/140cm and two pieces, at least 2½ x 3½in/6 x 9cm

▣ Fusible webbing
▣ Sashing: ¾yard/75cm
▣ Corner post: ¼yard/25cm
▣ Borders: ½yard/50cm, 60in/150cm wide fabric
▣ Backing: 55 x 55in/140 x 140cm
▣ Batting: 55 x 55in/140 x 140cm
▣ 9 buttons
▣ Binding: ½yard/50cm

CUTTING

These instructions are for one block.

1 From the house walls fabric, cut the following: one rectangle 4½ x 5½in/11.5 x 14cm; two strips, 1½in x 7½/4 x 19cm; two strips, 1½ x 4½in/4 x11.5 cm and six strips, 1½ x 2½in/4 x 6cm.

2 From the roof/chimney fabric, cut the following: two 3½in/9cm squares; two 2½in/6cm squares; two 1½in/4cm squares; two strips, 1½ x 3½in/4 x 9cm and one strip, 1½ x 4½in/4 x 11.5cm.

3 From the window fabrics, cut two strips, each 1½ x 13in/4 x 33cm.

4 From the door fabrics, cut one rectangle, 2½ x 4½in/6 x 11.5cm; two 1½in/4cm squares in a fabric to contrast with the door (for the porch) and one rectangle, 2 x 3in/5 x 7.5cm for the small arched window.

5 From the background fabric, cut two rectangles, 2½ x 3½in/6 x 9cm; two strips 1½ x 11½in/4 x 29cm; one strip 1½ x 4½in/4 x 11.5cm and two strips 1½ x 2½in/4 x 6cm.

6 From the ground fabric (or background fabric if not using a different pattern), one strip, 1½ x 12½in/4 x 32cm.

STITCHING

1 To make the windows, stitch together the two light strips along the long sides, right sides together. Press, then cut into eight 1½in/4cm segments, turn every other strip upside down and stitch into four-patch blocks (diagram 1). Make four altogether.

2 Stitch one of the 1½ x 2½in/ 4 x 6cm house walls strips between two window blocks, then two at either end. Repeat to make two units.

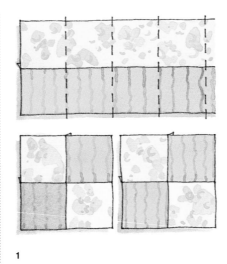

1

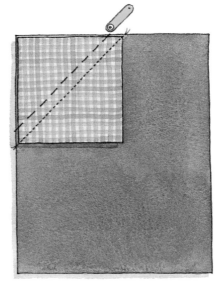

2

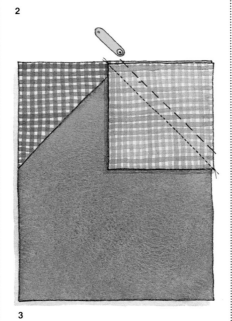

3

3 Stitch one of the 1½ x 7½in/ 19 x 4cm house walls strips to the left-hand side of one window unit and to the right side of the other.

4 To make the gable, place a 2½in/6cm roof fabric square over the 4½ x 5½in/11.5 x 14cm house walls rectangle, right sides together, aligning the top lefthand corner. Draw a diagonal line from the top right to bottom left of the roof fabric. Stitch along this line, then trim away the corner, leaving a ¼in/0.75cm seam (diagram 2). Press the seam towards the roof. Repeat for the other side of the rectangle (diagram 3). Press the seam as before.

5 Stitch the 1½ x 4½in/4 x 11.5cm strip of roof fabric across the top of the gable unit.

6 To make the door and porch, repeat steps 4 and 5, using the 2½ x 4½in/6 x 11.5cm door fabric rectangle and the two contrasting 1½in/4cm squares.

7 Stitch the remaining house wall fabric strips to either side of the door section (diagram 4).

8 Stitch the gable unit to the top of the door unit.

9 To make the roof and chimney, stitch together one of the background fabric rectangles (2½ x 3½in/6 x 9cm) and one of the 1½ x 3½in/4 x 9cm chimney fabric strips making a square. Repeat to make a second square.

10 Place this square over a 3½in/9cm roof fabric square, right sides together, making sure that the chimney strip lies horizontally across the top (diagram 5). Repeat.

11 Draw diagonal lines as shown in the diagram. Stitch on the lines, then

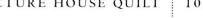

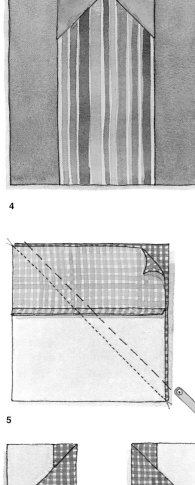

4

5

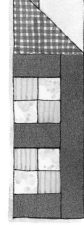

6

trim off the corners leaving a ¼in/0.75cm seam. Press open.

12 Stitch these to the window units, with the correct orientation for the roof slope on either side (diagram 6).

13 Stitch the center door/gable unit between the window units.

Arched window template

14 To make the chimney extensions, stitch a 1½in/4cm square of roof/chimney fabric to each end of the 4½in/11.5cm strip of background fabric, then add the 2½in/6cm strips of background fabric to either end of this piece.

15 Stitch this to the house block, matching seams for the chimney.

16 Add the side and bottom strips (diagram 7).

17 Repeat this process to make a total of nine blocks.

18 Trace the arched window and make a template from cardboard or plastic. Apply fusible webbing to the wrong side of the 2 x 3in/5 x 7.5cm

7

6   Stitch the borders to the quilt sides. Press the seams towards the borders.

7   Determine the length of the top and bottom borders by measuring the quilt top from side edge to side edge through the center. Cut two lengths from the border fabric to this measurement and 4½in/11.5cm wide.

8   Stitch the borders to the top and bottom edges of the quilt and press the seams towards the borders.

pieces. Trace around the template onto the paper back, cut out the arched shape, peel of the paper backing and apply to the block in the position indicated (diagram 7) with a hot iron. Stitch around the edges of the window with a close machine zig-zag.

ASSEMBLING

1   From the sashing fabric, cut twenty-four strips, each 2½ x 12½in/ 6 x 32cm. From the corner post fabric, cut sixteen 2½in/6cm squares.

2   Arrange the blocks as desired. Use six of the sashing strips to connect the blocks in three rows of three.

3   Make two long strips, each stitched with three sashing strips and two corner posts. Use these to stitch the three rows of blocks together, matching seams carefully.

4   Using the remaining sashing strips and corner posts, make outer sashing strips. Stitch to the top, bottom and sides of the quilt.

5   Determine the length of the two side borders by measuring the quilt top from top edge to bottom edge through the center. Cut two lengths from the border fabric to this measurement and 4½in/11.5cm wide.

FINISHING

1   Lay the backing right side down and smooth out any wrinkles. Center the batting on top, then the pieced top, leaving a small margin of batting and backing showing all around.

2   Baste or pin the fabric sandwich together (see page 37). Quilt by hand or machine following the line of the house blocks. Stitch a button to each of the door patches.

3   Cut strips of binding 2in/5cm wide to a total length of 212in/539cm and use to bind the quilt with a double-fold binding (see page 85).

Picture blocks often have a significance beyond their face value. Sailing ships, for example, indicate nautical connections and voyages. When Charles Lindbergh made his historic solo flight across the Atlantic in 1927, a quilt block of a plane became popular. They all speak of their makers' desire to record daily lives and combine an economical way of providing warmth with decorative textiles for their families and homes. Use these examples, or representational blocks of your own making, in place of the house in the quilt project.

Sailboats Pieced Block

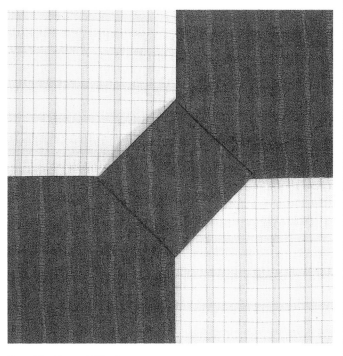

Bow Tie Pieced Block

Aeroplane Pieced Block

Basket Pieced Block

Aspirations Amish

THE AMISH – A RELIGIOUS SECT AND COMMUNITY RESIDING IN THE UNITED STATES – LEAD A LIFE OF SIMPLICITY WHICH REFLECTS THEIR BELIEFS AND STRONG SENSE OF CULTURE. THEIR QUILTS SHOW A DISTINCTIVE USE OF COLOR. THE QUILTS ARE OFTEN THOUGHT TO BE DARK BUT, IN FACT, BOTH LIGHT AND DARK FABRICS HAVE BEEN USED, CREATING A UNIQUE QUALITY THAT APPEARS TO GLOW FROM WITHIN. AMISH OR AMISH-LIKE QUILTS ARE BOTH SIMPLE AND BEAUTIFUL; THE DESIGNS USED CREATE LARGE AREAS BEGGING FOR EXTENSIVE QUILTING. THIS MEANS THAT THEY ARE QUICK TO PIECE, WHILE, AT THE SAME TIME, GIVING US AREAS TO QUILT, SO THAT WE CAN ALSO RELAX AND ENJOY THE PROCESS.

Quilt size: 60 x 60in/153 x 153cm

Materials

All fabrics used in the quilt are 45in/115cm wide, 100% cotton

◘ Fabrics for the top:

¾yard/75cm grey; 1yard/1m turquoise; 1½yards/1.5m brown; 2yards/2m purple; ¾yard/75cm navy

◘ Backing: 64 x 64in/163 x 163cm
◘ Batting: 2oz, 64 x 64in/163 x 163cm
◘ Quilting thread
◘ Hanging sleeve: 62 x 5in/157 x 13cm

CUTTING

1   Trace templates A to E from pages 112 and 113, then cut out in cardboard or template plastic, including seam allowances.

2   For the pieced top: using template A, cut one in grey, one in turquoise, one in purple and one in brown;
using template B, cut four in brown, twelve in turquoise;
using template C, cut eight in brown, four in purple, four in grey;
using template D, cut eight in grey, eight in purple;
using template E, cut eight in turquoise;
cut four 8½in/21.5cm squares in grey.

3   For the border, cut four strips, 2½ x 26in/6 x 66cm in brown; four strips, 2½ x 42in/6 x 107cm in brown and four strips, 8½ x 46in/21.5 x 117cm in purple. These pieces will be trimmed to fit at a later stage.

STITCHING

Follow the quilt assembly plan for color placement.

1   To create the blocks for the center diamond, take a "B" triangle and place it on top of an "A" square, right sides together and aligning raw edges (diagram 1). Stitch, taking a ¼in/0.75cm seam, then press the seam allowance towards the triangle.

2   Add a second "B" triangle to the opposite side of the square in the same way.

3   Stitch a third and fourth "B" triangle to the remaining two sides of the square. You now have a new square (diagram 2).

4   Using four "C" triangles, stitch them to the sides of the new square in the same way.

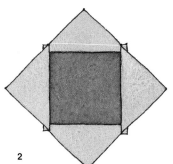

1

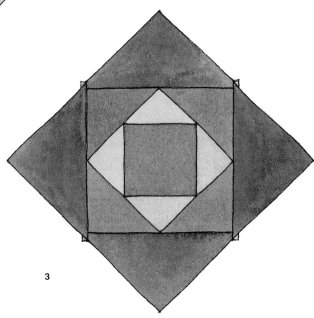

2

3

5   Repeat the procedure, this time using four "D" triangles (diagram 3). The block is now complete. Make three more blocks in the same way.

6   Stitch two blocks together and press the seams open.

7   Stitch the remaining two blocks together and press the seams open, then stitch the two pairs of blocks together to form one large square as shown on the quilt assembly plan. Press the seams open.

8   Measure the square from side edge to side edge through the center, then trim the four 26in/66cm brown border strips to this measurement.

9   Stitch a brown strip to two opposite sides of the square and press the seams towards the strip.

10   Stitch a turquoise "E" square to each end of the remaining brown strips, press the seam towards the strip, then stitch these to the remaining two sides of the square, matching seams.

11   Measure the new square from side edge to side edge through the center: it should be 26½in/67.25cm. Add ⅜in/1cm to this or to the dimension of your square, if different, and cut two navy squares to this measurement. Sub-cut each square in half on the diagonal to create four triangles.

12   Stitch the navy triangles, one to each side of the pieced square and borders.

3 Lay the quilt right side up and sew lines of basting 2 to 3in/5 to 8cm apart across the quilt from top to bottom and side to side. Now bring the backing fabric over the batting onto the top and baste to hold in place. This will trap the batting and keep it clean, which is important as the quilt will be handled a great deal during quilting.

4

4 Hand-quilt along the marked design, then remove all basting threads and trim the backing and batting to extend ½in/1.5cm beyond the quilt top.

5 Bind the quilt with a double-fold binding. The excess batting and backing are used to increase the bulk within the binding (diagram 5).

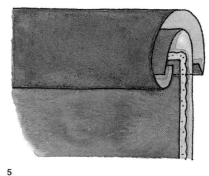

5

6 Attach a hanging sleeve (see page 23) and label your quilt.

13 Measure the sides of the new square and trim the four 42in/107cm brown border strips to this measurement.

14 Stitch these four strips and the remaining four turquoise "E" squares to the pieced square as in steps 9 and 10.

15 Measure the sides of the new square and trim the four purple border strips to this measurement.

16 Stitch these four strips and the four grey squares to the pieced square as described in steps 9 and 10.

FINISHING

1 Lightly press the pieced top, then mark the center diamond with the quilting designs from page 43 enlarged to fit (diagram 4). Mark a 1in/2.5cm grid on the large navy triangles. Mark the feather design from page 42 enlarged to fit on the borders.

Tip *Use a thin sliver of soap to mark a quilt: it can easily be sponged off after quilting and it eases the needle through the fabric as you quilt.*

2 Lay out the backing, smoothing out any wrinkles, and lay the batting on top, aligning raw edges.

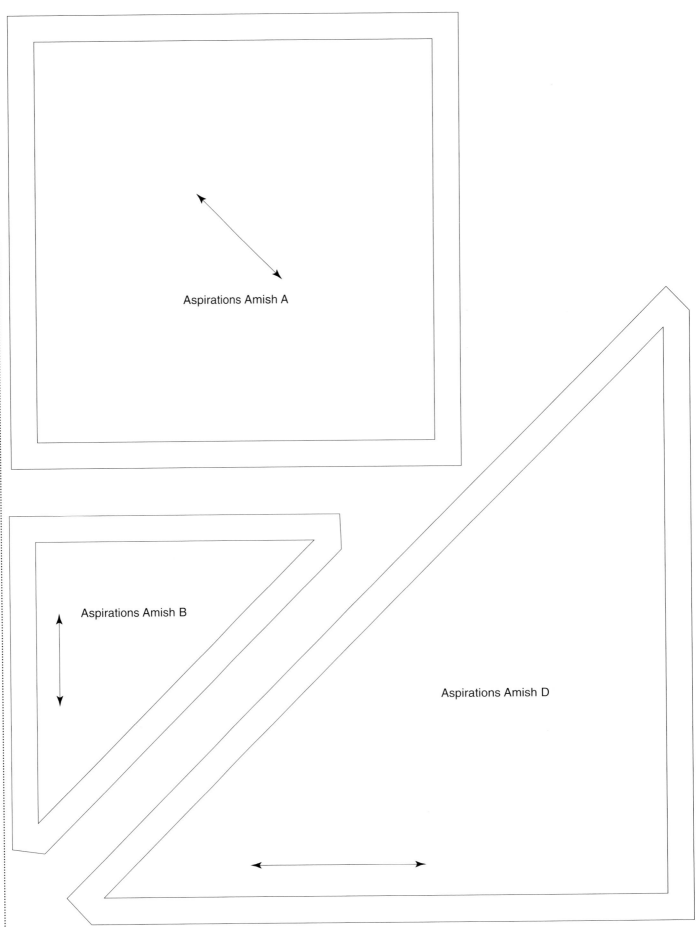

Aspirations Amish A

Aspirations Amish B

Aspirations Amish D

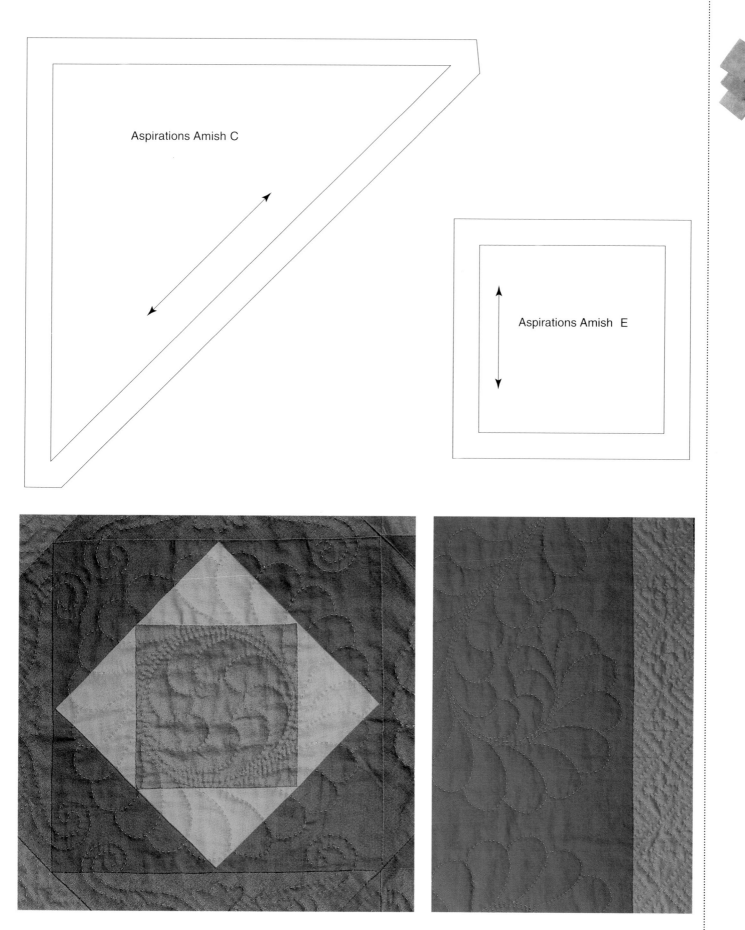

Aspirations Amish C

Aspirations Amish E

3D OR ILLUSION PATCHWORK

DESIGN

Working to produce the illusion of three dimensions on the flat surface of a quilt can be fascinating and provide the quiltmaker with endless possibilities for creating interesting and striking designs. The effects of depth, distance and movement are created through the choice of shape and fabric tones.

Tumbling Blocks

A number of traditional patterns are based on simple shapes, such as hexagons, diamonds and triangles, which are easily drawn on isometric paper and make a good starting point from which to explore three dimensional design.

1   Draw a hexagon. Find the center point and draw lines from here to alternate points to create three diamonds. This is the base for the traditional "Tumbling Blocks" or "Baby Blocks" design. You can see at this stage that you have drawn a square box.

2   Use a soft lead pencil to shade one diamond dark, one light and one medium. It will now appear as though a light is shining on one side of the box, putting the other two in the shade. The boxes "tessellate" (see page 70) but the "light" must always fall on the same side of all the blocks.

3   Experiment first with this box shape by extending the parallel lines to make long, tall and flat shapes. Each of these will tessellate but it is interesting to combine two, drawing in connecting shapes if necessary.

4   Move onto other shapes – split diamonds, squares, triangles and rectangles – by drawing lines to the corners from the center point or an off-center point. Use shading in the subdivisions to create 3D effects. For shapes with four angles, you will need to shade four tones.

Floating Shapes

Try superimposing one shape on another, for example, a triangle on a hexagon or another triangle, a square on a rotated square. You will notice that there are gaps between one part of the design and the other. If these are shaded very dark, it will seem as if your design is floating, that you are looking into space beyond.

Setting In

Try setting in one shape to another, e.g. a box into a hexagon, a diamond into a diamond, a square into a rotated square.

It is also possible to create the impression of looking into a box by shading the center darker than the surrounding areas.

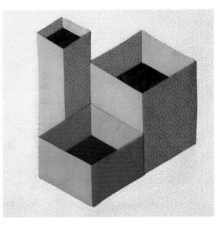

Try this with other shapes. Choose the "block" you find most interesting and use it to draw an all-over pattern. When translating this into patchwork, of course, you will need to make the overall shape of the patchwork top square or rectangular, thus making it necessary to make extra templates. Many of the straight-sided designs you have been working with could be drawn using curves. So long as the curves are not too deep, they should not pose problems making up the designs in fabric.

Interesting 3D borders can enhance an illusion quilt, whether or not you use the same shapes as in the central design. Always plan the border alongside the main part of the work, to get the right balance and to help you to work out fabric amounts.

Attic Windows

This idea of darker fabrics producing an effect of depth is taken a stage further in the traditional "Attic Windows" design, by the addition of lines that give the impression that the work is viewed from the side. The "windows" must contrast in tone or color to the sills and sides. Since, generally speaking, warm colors appear to advance and cool ones recede, placing blue in the "window" and surrounding it with warm colors will give an even greater illusion of depth or sky beyond. A more solid-looking "Attic Windows" block has surrounding strips, which strengthens it even more.

It is fascinating to experiment with fabrics you might use in the "windows". Try motifs cut from a print fabric – flowers, cats, birds or fish, for example.

A small patchwork block can be used in this position. Or you could cut up a pre-printed picture or one you have made yourself and place the sections in the windows, allowing the frames to "hide" some parts of the picture. This will give the impression that you are looking through a series of windows onto a landscape or scene.

Adventurous quilters can experiment with textured fabrics, such as bobbly wools or sheers, though only for a wallhanging, they would not be practical for a bed quilt.

The following quilt project also explores this design.

Log Cabin

"Log Cabin" and "Courthouse Steps" are two other traditional patterns with which you can practise tonal effects. Use a brightly colored central square (or other shape) and grade the strips from light to dark (see also the quilt project on page 120). Experiment with the "Log Cabin" technique based on shapes other than a square, such as triangles, rectangles or hexagons.

FABRICS

Choosing fabrics for this type of design should be done with tonal contrast very firmly in mind. The greater the contrast, the stronger will be the three dimensional image. Black, white and yellow, for example, would give a contemporary look with great impact. It is also possible, however, to create a gentle scheme where contrasts are not so marked but still achieve the desired effect (as in the Tumbling Blocks Crib Quilt on page 46).

Care should be taken not to place two patches of equal value together, as this would change the pattern and spoil the effect. Sometimes this can be avoided by using another color but there must be more of this color else-where in the patchwork.

If you would like to use multi-colored scraps in a block quilt with a design such as "Attic Windows", a single color used in the same focal point in each block throughout the work will act as a unifying element. Otherwise it might look confused. This is true in the case of a "Log Cabin" quilt, where the red center in the blocks brings order to the design and rests the eye.

Check first that each block works in the way you want it to. An excellent way of doing this is to make tiny templates to scale and use them to cut shapes from the fabrics, which have been sorted into light, medium and dark tones. Stick them onto cardboard. This gives you the effect of a distance view of the full-scale block.

Better still, make a small-scale collage of the whole quilt. Draw a scale outline of the quilt on graph or isometric paper, mark it off into blocks and build up the color plan using the small templates. Start in the center and work outwards to the borders. The collage takes a little time to complete but has huge advantages, the main one being that you will see exactly what the quilt will look like before beginning to sew, giving you the opportunity at an early stage to experiment and substitute fabrics where necessary. You will also find it easier to work out fabric amounts.

CONSTRUCTION

Designing patchwork has to be done with the practical constraints of stitching in mind. In 3D work, you will often find corners need to be "set-in" (see page 13). Occasionally you will want to set in a corner where there is no seam, so one must be created. This can distract from the design but can be disguised by the use of strip patchwork or simply by quilting in the direction of the extra seam, making it part of the quilting design.

Attic Windows Quilt

LARGE SCRAPS WERE USED FOR THIS QUILT BUT WERE RESTRICTED TO THREE COLORS. BLUE WINDOWS THROUGHOUT GIVE COHESION TO THE DESIGN, WHILE THE USE OF PURPLE AND YELLOW-ORANGE, EACH IN TWO VALUES, MAKES AN INTERESTING AND LIVELY CONTRAST, WITHOUT LOOKING CONFUSED. THE EFFECT OF DEPTH ACHIEVED THROUGH THE TONALITY OF THE FABRICS IS FURTHER ENHANCED BY QUILTING LINES WHICH FOLLOW THE DIRECTION OF THE "LIGHT" ON THE LEDGES AND SIDES OF THE WINDOWS. THE BORDERS AND BINDINGS ARE CUT FROM TWO FABRICS USED IN THE CENTRAL AREA.

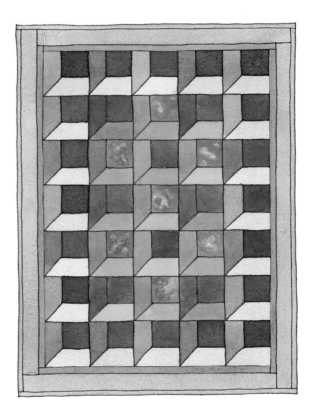

Quilt size: 36 x 48in/92 x 122cm

Materials

All fabrics used in the quilt top are 45in/115cm wide
- ▣ Large scraps of cotton fabric, totalling:
  - ½yd/41cm in dark and dark-medium blues;
  - ¼yd/23cm in medium purples;
  - ¼yd/23cm in medium oranges;
  - ¼yd/23cm in light purples;
  - ¼yd/23cm in light oranges

- ▣ Borders and binding: for each border, use one of the above fabrics. You will need the following amounts in addition to the above:
  - inner borders: ¼yd/114 x 13cm;
  - outer borders and binding: 18 x 50in/45 x 127cm
- ▣ Backing: 40 x 51in/102 x 130cm
- ▣ Batting: 2oz, 38 x 48in/98 x 122cm
- ▣ Clear nylon machine-quilting thread
- ▣ Cotton-covered thread in medium blue, yellow and purple

CUTTING

Tip *As you cut, lay the patches on the floor or onto a wall-mounted pinboard, following the quilt assembly plan. For the sides and ledges, cut only one or two pieces from each fabric at a time, until you get a clearer picture of how your colors will balance. At the same time, check that each window is producing the effect of depth that you need.*

1   From the blue fabrics, cut strips 4in/10cm wide, then sub-cut into 35 4in/10cm squares.

2   From the medium purples, cut strips 2⅞in/7cm wide, then use template A on the back of the material to mark and cut 20 pieces (diagram 1). Do not turn the template over.

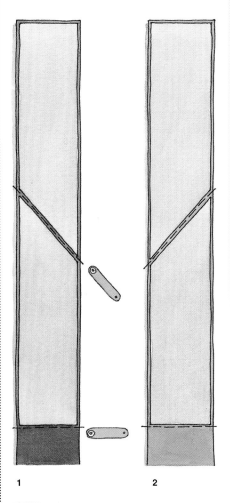

1

2

3   From the medium oranges, cut strips 2⅞in/7cm wide, then cut 15 pieces as before using the same side of the template.

4   From the light fabrics, cut strips 2⅞in/7cm wide, then reverse the template and cut 20 pieces from the light purples and 15 from the light oranges (diagram 2).

5   For the inner border, from your chosen fabric, cut two strips, 1¼ x 44in/3 x 112 cm, and two strips 1¼ x 31½in/3 x 80cm.

6   For the outer border, from your chosen fabric, cut two strips, 3 x 50in/ 7.5 x 127cm, and two strips 3 x 38in/7.5 x 96cm.

7   For the binding, from your chosen fabric, cut four strips, 1¼ x 38in/3 x 127cm.

STITCHING

1   Start with the top row of your arrangement. With right sides together, pin and stitch a square to a side piece for each block in this row, stopping the seam at the seam allowance (diagram 3).

2   Stitch the ledge to the bottom edge of each square, again stopping the seam at the seam allowance (diagram 4).

3   Place the diagonal edges right sides together and stitch the seam right to the outer corner, beginning exactly where you stopped the last line of stitching. Press the seams open.

4   Repeat for each row of the arrangement.

5   Stitch the blocks into rows and press the seams open, then stitch the rows together. Press these seams, then iron the front of the work very lightly.

ADDING THE BORDERS

1   Measure the quilt from side to side through the center, then cut one of the shorter inner border strips to this measurement. Pin and stitch to the top of the quilt.

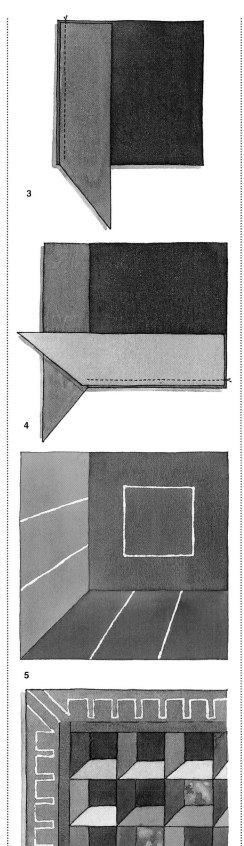

3

4

5

6

Attic Windows A

2   Measure the quilt from top to bottom through the center, then cut one of the longer inner border strips to this measurement. Pin and stitch to the side of the quilt.

3   Continue in this way, adding the remaining two inner border and the four outer border strips in a log cabin arrangement, following the quilt assembly plan.

FINISHING

1   Mark the patchwork top for quilting as shown in diagram 5. Cut a 1½in/4cm square from template cardboard or plastic and use to mark the border with the quilting design shown in diagram 6.

2   Lay out the backing, smoothing out any wrinkles, and center the batting on top.

3   Lay the pieced top, right side up, and sew lines of basting about 4in/11cm apart across the quilt from top to bottom and side to side through all three layers.

4   To machine-quilt, start by making several small stitches very close together, then alter the stitch size to

medium and stitch to the end of the line. Finish with a few closely worked stitches. Trim off the excess thread on the front and back of the work or, if you prefer, take the threads to the back of the work, tie and trim. With colored thread in the bobbin and nylon thread on the spool, machine-quilt "in-the-ditch" around all the blocks and between the two borders.

5   Using blue thread on the spool, quilt the marked squares in each "window". Use purple thread to quilt

the marked lines on the sides and ledges of the outer window blocks and yellow-orange to complete the inner window blocks.

6   Quilt each border in a continuous line, then quilt the diagonal lines on the corners.

7   When all the quilting has been completed, trim off the excess batting and backing, then bind with a double-fold binding.

Log Cabin Quilt

THIS QUILT FEATURES FOUNDATION PIECING, A METHOD WHICH ALLOWS ACCURATE PIECING OF GEOMETRIC DESIGNS. THE PIECES ARE STITCHED TO SQUARES OF LIGHTWEIGHT COTTON FABRIC. THIS DOES ADD EXTRA WEIGHT, SO THAT BATTING IS NOT NECESSARY. AN ALTERNATIVE IS TO USE A SPECIAL PAPER AS THE FOUNDATION (PAGE 11), WHICH CAN BE TORN AWAY ONCE THE PIECING IS COMPLETE. THE "LOG CABIN" DESIGN IS ONE OF THE QUINTESSENTIAL DESIGNS FOR SCRAP QUILTS. MANY FABRICS CAN BE USED AS LONG AS THE LIGHT AND DARK ARRANGEMENT IS FOLLOWED. THERE ARE MANY DIFFERENT WAYS IN WHICH BLOCKS CAN BE SET TOGETHER. I'VE USED THE TRADITIONAL "BARN RAISING".

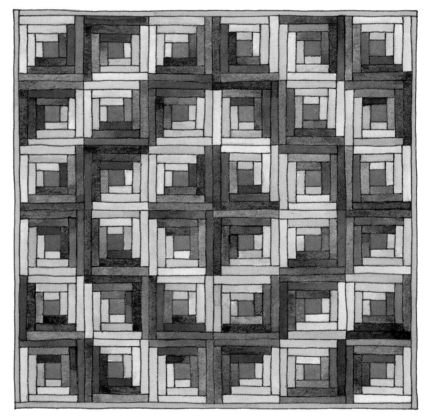

Quilt size: 60 x 60in/144 x 144cm
Finished block size: 10in/24cm

Materials

- Foundation fabric: 3yards/3m (or equivalent to give 36 12in/30cm squares) lightweight cotton in white or cream, 60in/155cm wide
- Centers: ½yard/45cm red fabric
- Light strips: scrap fabrics to a total of 2yards/2m (strips are cut 1¾in/4.5 wide, so any pieces larger than 1¾ x 20in/ 4.5 x 51cm would be big enough for the longest strips)

- Dark strips: scrap fabrics to a total of 2yards/2m (see above)
- Backing: 3¾yards/3.5m flannel in a color to harmonize with the light and dark strips
- Batting (optional): low loft, 65 x 65in/165 x 165cm
- Quilting thread: variegated machine embroidery thread

CUTTING

1   Cut the foundation fabric into thirty-six 12in/30cm squares. Lightly press two diagonal creases, so that you can mark the centers.

2   From the red fabric, cut thirty-six 3in/7.5cm squares.

STITCHING

1   Position a red square in the center of a foundation square, by lining up a corner on each creased line. Press and pin to secure the two layers.

2   Using a light fabric to begin with, cut two strips of the same fabric, 1¾ x 3in/4.5 x 7.5cm and 1¾ x 4¼in/4.5 x 10.5cm. Place the shorter strip, right side down, against one edge of the red center, aligning the raw edges. Stitch through all three layers, taking a ¼in/0.75cm seam allowance (diagram 1). Remove the pin.

3   Fold the strip over to reveal the right side of the fabric and press it flat against the foundation.

4   Place the second light strip along the righthand edge, right side down, and stitch as before (diagram 2).

5   Fold the second light strip over and press flat against the foundation.

6   Select dark fabrics for the other two sides of the center square. Cut two strips 1¾ x 4¼in/4.5 x 10.5cm and 1¾ x 5½in/13.5cm. Add the two dark strips along the bottom edge and the lefthand edge as before. The first round of strips is now complete, establishing the sequencing of the light and dark fabrics (diagram 3).

7   Add two more rounds of strips, increasing the lengths of the strips by 1¼in/3cm every alternate one to accommodate the growing size of the block.

8   When the block is complete, trim the foundation fabric level with the edge of the last round of strips on all four sides (diagram 4). Make a total of thirty-six blocks in this way.

9   Following the quilt assembly plan, arrange the blocks into the "Barn Raising" pattern and stitch them together by placing the blocks right sides together and stitching through all layers. Press the seams open as you work to reduce bulk.

Tip   *You may find it easier to stitch the blocks into sets of four before stitching the rows together.*

ASSEMBLING

1   Cut the flannel backing in half crosswise, then trim off the selvages, as it tends to pull and may pucker the center seam.

2   Stitch the two halves together down the selvage edge. Press the quilt top and backing.

3   Smooth the backing and the pieced top, wrong sides together, centering the seam in the backing. If you are using batting, smooth it between the top and backing at this stage. The batting should extend beyond the quilt top by at least 2in/5cm on all sides.

4   Baste the layers together in a vertical and horizontal grid through the centers of each block and around the outer edges.

5   Trim the backing to extend beyond the quilt top by at least 3½in/9cm on all sides.

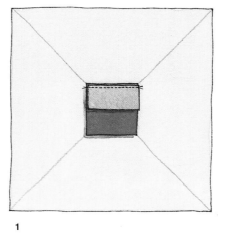

1

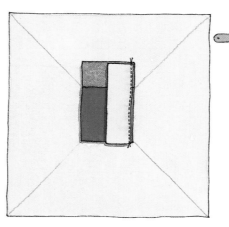

2

3

4

FINISHING

1   Using the machine embroidery thread, machine-quilt down both sides of each of the seams joining the blocks, ¼in/0.75cm away from the seams, both vertically and horizontally.

2   Using a removable fabric marker, mark diagonal lines in both directions across the block centers, then quilt along these lines.

3   Trim the backing fabric to extend 2½in/6cm beyond the quilt top on all four sides and, if using batting, trim this to extend ½in/1.5cm beyond the edge of the quilt top.

4   Fold the outer edge of the backing to meet the edge of the quilt top and press the fold.

5   Fold again so that the edge of the fold covers ¼in/0.75cm of the quilt top and pin this double fold along the edge of the quilt top. Baste to secure. Clip away the fabric behind the fold at the corners to reduce bulk (diagrams 5a, b and c).

6   Hand-hem the corners, then machine the backing down to the quilt top all around the edge.

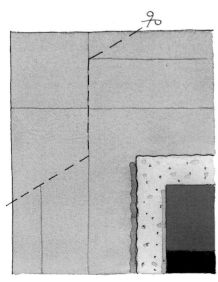

5a

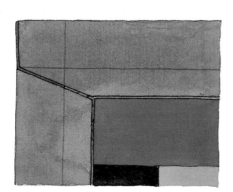

5b

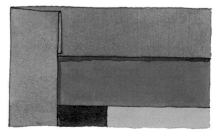

5c

Star Crazy Quilt

ANOTHER QUILT DESIGN WHICH CAN BE MADE USING THE BASIC FOUNDATION PIECING TECHNIQUE IS THE CRAZY QUILT. TRADITIONALLY, THIS WAS MADE WITH A VARIETY OF EXOTIC FABRICS, SUCH AS SILK AND SATIN. THE FOUNDATION SQUARES SERVE TO STABILIZE THESE FABRICS, WHICH ARE SOMETIMES RATHER STRETCHY AND DIFFICULT TO CONTROL. CRAZY BLOCKS WERE OFTEN RICHLY EMBROIDERED OVER THE SEAMS AND HAD SENTIMENTAL MEMENTOES AND MOTIFS COVERING MUCH OF THE QUILT SURFACE. IN THIS CONTEMPORARY EXAMPLE, SMALL STARS HAVE BEEN APPLIQUÉD ONTO THE PATCHES WITH HAND-SEWN BUTTONHOLE STITCH. EACH BLOCK HAS A RED SILK DIAMOND AT ITS CENTER AND I'VE USED A COMBINATION OF SILK, SATIN AND COTTON FABRICS.

Quilt size: 35 x 35in/89 x 89cm Block size: 9in/23cm

Materials

All fabrics used in the quilt top are 45in/115cm wide

- ▣ Foundation fabric: 1yard/1m lightweight cotton in white or cream
- ▣ Diamonds: ¼yard/23cm red silk
- ▣ Scrap fabrics: a total of 1½ – 2yards/1.5 – 1.75m of assorted silks and cottons (as the color scheme is random, you can always add to the basic amount)
- ▣ Fusible webbing

- ▣ Stars and binding strips: 3in/7.5cm wide strips in a variety of bright, plain cotton fabrics
- ▣ Embroidery thread: red size 8 pearl cotton
- ▣ Borders and sashing: ¾yard/0.75m black cotton fabric
- ▣ Backing: a piece of cotton fabric, 1yard/1m square
- ▣ Batting: low loft, 1yard/1m square
- ▣ 9 pearl buttons

CUTTING

1 Cut nine 10in/25cm squares from the foundation fabric. Press a horizontal and vertical crease in each one to establish the centers.

2 Trace template A (page 127), then transfer to thin cardboard or template plastic and cut out. Using the template, cut nine diamonds from the red silk.

STITCHING

1 Position a diamond at the center of a foundation square and pin.

2 Cut a random shape from one of the scrap fabrics, which has at least one side longer than the side of the diamond. Position this, right side down, on top of one side of the diamond. Stitch along the edge through the three layers of fabric. Begin and end the stitching line at each end of the diamond shape (diagram 1). Remove the pin.

3 Flip the patch over, so that it lies flat against the foundation and the right side of the fabric is showing. Press.

4 Place a ruler along the straight edges of the diamond and draw a line over the patch, so that the edges of diamond extend along the side of the patch (diagram 2). Use scissors to trim the patch on these lines.

5 Cut another random shape from a different scrap, which has at least one side longer than the side of the diamond and the first shape. Place this along the second side of the diamond and stitch down as before (diagram 3). Flip over and trim. Press. When adding the patches, it is better to be generous with the size until they are stitched down, then, when they have been flipped and pressed, they can be trimmed to the desired size and shape. For visual interest within each block, vary the shape and sizes of the patches.

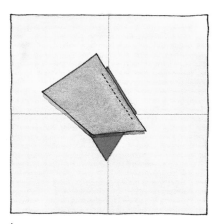

1

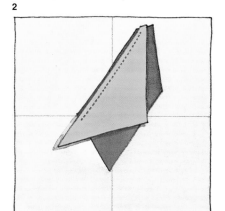

2

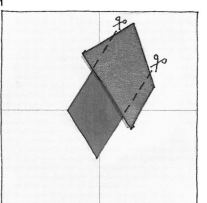

3

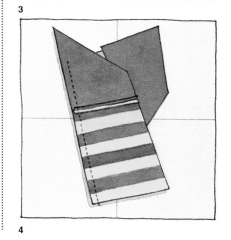

4

6 Continue to add patches, right side down, stitch, flip and trim until the foundation fabric is completely covered.

7 There is a tendency for the last few patches to become rather large as the straight edges get longer. If you prefer smaller patches, just piece a few fabrics together, then treat these as one patch and add to the block (diagram 4).

8 Press, taking care with the heat of the iron on delicate fabrics. Trim the block to an exact 9½in/24.5cm square.

9 Stitch all around the outer edges of the blocks to secure the patches to the foundation square. Make a total of nine blocks in this way.

ADDING THE STARS

1 Cut twenty-seven or more 2½in/6cm squares of fusible webbing and the same number of squares in the plain star fabrics.

2 Trace and make a cardboard or plastic template from shape B (page 127).

3 Draw around the template onto the paper backing of the fusible webbing. Cut out the star shapes. Peel off the paper backing and iron down the star shapes onto the blocks. Place three or more on each block.

4 Buttonhole stitch by hand around the outer edges of each star using the pearl cotton.

ADDING SASHING STRIPS AND BORDERS

1 From the black fabric, cut six strips, 2 x 9½in/5 x 24.5cm.

2 Join the blocks in sets of three with sashing strips between them.

3 Cut two more sashing strips 2in/5cm wide by the total length of the joined blocks. Stitch the sashing strips between the three rows of blocks to complete the center panel of the quilt (diagram 5).

5

4 Determine the length of the top and bottom borders by measuring the quilt top from side edge to side edge through the center. Cut two lengths from the border fabric to this measurement and 3½in/9cm wide.

5 Stitch these to the top and bottom of the quilt.

6 Determine the length of the side borders by measuring the quilt top from top edge to bottom edge through the center. Cut two lengths from the border fabric to this measurement and 3½in/9cm wide. Stitch to the quilt.

FINISHING

1 Spread the backing, right side down, on the work surface, then smooth the batting and the quilt top, right side up, on top.

2 Pin, then sew lines of basting about 4in/11cm apart across the quilt from top to bottom and side to side.

3 Sew a pearl button into the center of each of the red silk diamonds.

4 Machine-quilt the sashing strips and borders close to the seams. Quilt over the blocks in zig-zag line to reflect the shapes of the patches.

5 Trim the borders, batting and backing down to 2½in/6cm at the top and righthand side and 3in/7.5cm at the bottom and lefthand side of the quilt, or as desired.

6 Cut binding strips from the plain fabric, 2½in/6cm wide and in random lengths.

7 Making an angled seam (see page 21), piece together three or four strips in different colors to create sufficient lengths to bind the edges.

8 Fold the binding strip in half lengthwise, wrong sides together, and use to bind the quilt with a double-fold binding (see page 85).

Diamond A

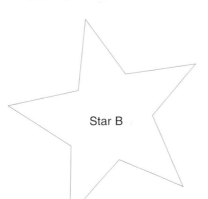

Star B

MINIATURE QUILTS

Small versions of full-size quilts are fun to make as gifts or to decorate the home. As they do not represent as much of an investment in either time or resources as larger projects, they can be made to try out color schemes or design ideas that you are considering for bigger quilts. When working small, however, the margin for error is much less and this will sharpen up your piecing skills. A successful result relies on accurate cutting and an exact ¼in/0.75cm seam allowance. When looking for suitable blocks to scale down, choose those without too many separate pieces and which can, if possible, use rotary cutting and quick piecing techniques (see pages 80 to 81).

When cutting border strips, allow extra width beyond the finished size and seam allowance, then trim down after the borders have been stitched to the main panel. This helps to create straighter border strips.

The three quilts illustrated here are very small scale, no wider than 7in/18cm. The two projects which follow are on a slightly larger scale. Both use ingenious quick piecing techniques to assemble the miniature patches.

Windmill Mini Quilt

Hearts Shadow Appliqué Mini Quilt

Double Wedding Ring Mini Quilt

Amish Mini Quilt

PLAIN COLORED TRIANGLES IN TWO SIZES ARE COMBINED WITH BLACK, GIVING THE CHARACTERISTIC COLORING OF A TRADITIONAL AMISH QUILT (SEE ALSO PAGE 109). THE CENTER PANEL IS FRAMED BY THREE BORDERS. THERE ARE TWO VERSIONS IN THE PHOTOGRAPH, ONE QUILTED BY HAND AND ONE BY MACHINE. THE CHOICE IS YOURS.

Quilt size: 14 x 16in/35.5 x 40cm

Materials

- Cotton fabrics: twelve 4in/10cm squares in assorted plain colors
- Black fabric: ½yard/45cm
- Borders and binding: 2in/5cm wide strips to a total length of 65in/165cm in two different plain colors
- Backing: cotton fabric, 16 x 18in/35.5 x 45.5cm
- Batting: low loft, 16 x 18in/35.5 x 45.5cm

CUTTING

1   Cut six 3½in/9cm squares from plain colors. Divide these into triangles by cutting across one diagonal.

2   From the remaining plain colors, cut six more squares, 2¼in/5.5cm.

3   From the black fabric, cut thirty-six squares, 2¼in/5.5cm.

STITCHING

1   Place each of the six smaller colored squares with a black square, right sides together.

2   Draw a diagonal line across each pair, then stitch ¼in/0.75cm away down both sides of this line (diagram 1).

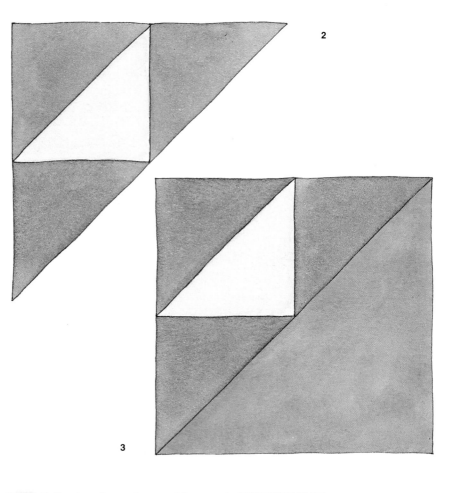

2

3

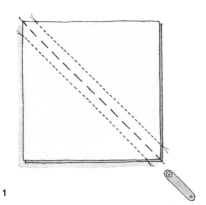

1

3   Cut on the marked line. Trim the seam allowance to ⅛in/3mm (no less) and cut off the projecting corners to reduce bulk. This makes twelve two-colored squares.

4   Cut the remaining black squares into two triangles each by cutting across one diagonal.

5   To each two-colored square, stitch two black triangles (diagram 2). Trim the seam allowances as before.

6   Complete the blocks by stitching a larger colored triangle to each of the triangles just made (diagram 3).

7   Following the quilt assembly plan, stitch the blocks together, so that you have four rows of three blocks.

ADDING THE BORDERS

1   From the black fabric, cut strips 2in/5cm wide and long enough to fit the sides, top and bottom of the quilt.

2   Stitch the borders to the sides first, then to the top and bottom of the quilt. Trim the borders to measure 1¼in/3.75cm wide.

3   From the border fabric, cut strips 1½in/4cm wide and long enough to fit the sides, top and bottom of the quilt. Stitch to the quilt as before, then trim back to ¾in/2.25cm.

4   From the black fabric, cut strips 2½in/6cm wide and long enough to fit the sides, top and bottom of the quilt. Stitch to the quilt as before.

FINISHING

1   Lay the backing, batting and quilt top on a flat surface and baste the layers together in a grid.

2   Working by hand or machine, quilt in-the-ditch (see page 40) between the seams joining the blocks and along the borders. Contour quilt (see page 40) the colored triangles.

3   Trim the outer border, excess batting and backing to 1½in/4cm through all layers. Cut the binding strips to fit the four sides plus seam allowances.

4   Fold the binding strips in half lengthwise, wrong sides together and use to bind the quilt with a double-fold binding (see page 23).

Mini Trip Around the World

An ingenious method of strip piecing, similar to the Bargello method described on page 143, has been adapted to create this popular traditional design. The design is sometimes called "Sunshine and Shadow" by the Amish.

Quilt size: 14 x 14in/35.5 x 35.5cm

Materials

- Rotary cutter and mat
- Center panel fabrics: ⅛yard/12cm each of seven coordinating light and dark cotton print fabrics, 36in/90cm wide
- Border: ⅓yard/30cm cotton, 36in/90cm wide
- Batting: low loft, 16 x 16in/40 x 40cm
- Backing: 16 x 16in/40 x 40cm, cotton

CUTTING

1   Using a rotary cutter and mat, cut the fabrics for the center panel across the width of the fabric exactly 1½in/4cm wide.

STITCHING

1   Arrange the strips in a color sequence, either blending them from light to dark or alternating darks and lights.

2   Stitch strip 1 to strip 2 along one long side. As the strips are to be sub-cut into sections, use a smaller stitch than normal to prevent the seams coming undone. Press the seams either open or to one side as preferred.

3   Stitch strip 3 to strip 2, sewing the seam from the opposite direction.

4   Stitch the remainder of the strips together in the same way, alternating the direction of the seams so that the piece does not become distorted. Then place the top and bottom strip, right sides together, pin and stitch, so that the strips now form a tube. Press the final seam.

5   Place the tube flat on the cutting mat and trim the lefthand edge (see page 80).

6   Cut the tube into rings, 1½in/4cm wide. You can use the grid on the ruler or the cutting mat for this but you must cut even, accurate widths.

ASSEMBLING

1   As you will see from diagram 1, the quilt is divided into four sections. Start with section A which includes the center square of the quilt and is therefore the largest. Work from the center line out towards the lefthand side. Identify which is to be the key fabric (marked) – this can be the darkest, lightest or brightest fabric, as you choose.

key

1

2   Take one of the rings of fabrics and unpick the short seam closest to the key fabric and lay the strip on a flat surface with the key fabric at the top.

3   Take a second ring and unpick the seam which is second from the key fabric, so that when placed next to the first strip the key fabric is dropped by one square.

4   Contine to unpick rings dropping down a square from the key fabric each time, until seven strips are prepared.

5   Stitch these strips together, matching the seams exactly and using diagram 1 as a guide to the positioning of the key fabric, which should run diagonally across section A from top right to bottom left.

6   Section B requires six strips. Working from the center out to the right side and noting that the key fabric begins one down from the top, unpick the seams, lay out the strips in the correct sequence and stitch them together.

7   When section B is completed, stitch it to section A along the center seam, taking care to match all the small seams.

8   Make section C with seven strips and section D with six strips in the same way, using diagram 1 to position the key fabric. As you have already included the horizontal center line of the quilt in sections A and B, you must unpick and discard one square from each strip before stitching them together. This must come from the

opposite end of each strip as it is unpicked: make sure you take it from the right end.

9 When sections C and D are complete, stitch them together at the center seam, the stitch A/B to C/D.

ADDING THE BORDERS

1 From the border fabric, cut strips 2½in/6cm wide and long enough to fit the sides of the quilt plus a little more than the width of each strip, to allow for the mitered corners.

2 Join border strips to the top and bottom of the quilt, then to each side, mitering the corners as you work (see page 21).

FINISHING

1 Cut a piece of batting and backing ½-1in/1.5-2.5cm larger all around than the quilt top.

2 Lay the batting on the work surface, then place the backing on top, right side up and finally the quilt top, right side down, in the center. Smooth the three layers together and pin.

3 With the quilt top uppermost, stitch the three layers together around all four sides, taking a ¼in/0.75cm seam allowance and leaving a gap in one of the sides. Carefully clip away the excess batting close to the seam and trim the seams and corners to reduce bulk.

4 Turn the quilt to the right side. Push out the corners to sharp right angles and press so that the outer seam is lying along the very edges of the quilt. Slipstitch the gap closed.

5 Smooth and pin or baste the layers together. Quilt in diagonal lines across the squares in both directions by hand or machine. Quilt the borders following the seam lines.

SEMINOLE QUILTS

The Seminole Indians of the Florida Everglades employ bright, geometric bands of pattern to decorate their traditional garments. Although intricate to look at, the patterns are actually quite simple to produce and are all achieved by seaming strips of fabric together, then cutting and rearranging these cut segments. The complexity of the patterns varies according to the number of strips used, the color combinations employed and the angle at which the band is cut.

This is an ideal technique for the rotary cutter. Chain piecing will also speed up the sewing process and conserve thread.

FABRICS

Traditionally, the Seminoles use plain cottons but with the huge array of fabrics available, it is worth trying out mottled, hand-dyed fabrics or subtle tone-on-tone prints. Avoid large-scale prints as these tend to blur the effect. Tonal value is also important, as the placement of tones can cause an area to stand out or recede in a design.

DESIGN

Patterns may be worked to any size, provided the proportions remain constant. I experiment with paper to try different sizes and colorways before cutting into the fabric. I cut paper strips to the finished size, i.e. without seam allowance, then glue them onto a background before cutting and rearranging the segments.

Technical Terms

Strip: a single piece of fabric cut from selvage to selvage
Band: two or more strips seamed together
Segment: a unit produced by cutting across the width of the band – at right angles or with a 45° or 60° angle.

CONSTRUCTING PATTERNS

Strips should be cut from dressweight cotton and on the straight of grain. Allow a $\frac{1}{4}$in/0.75cm seam allowance on either side. When the band is cut into segments, include a $\frac{1}{4}$in/0.75cm seam allowance on either side again. Place the strips on your work surface in the order in which they are to be sewn.

Note   If working to a small scale, trim the seams after stitching to avoid too much bulk.

Use a small stitch length to avoid the seams unravelling when the band is cut into segments. Use a neutral thread to tone in with all the colors or use the main color in the bobbin and change the top color to match the strips.

When stitching, sew neighbouring strips in alternate directions to avoid the band curving. Press all seam allowances in a band in one direction but if joining two bands, press the seams of one band towards the top and the seams of the other towards the bottom. This is important when joining segments because the seam allowances will then lie in opposite directions and you will be able to match up and join units more accurately.

Checkerboard Pattern

You will need two fabrics of contrasting colors: A and B.

1   Cut three strips of uniform width from both fabrics. i.e. finished size plus seam allowances, for example, $2\frac{1}{2}$in/6.5cm wide.

2   Arrange these in two groups of three strips. Join the strips into two bands, taking a $\frac{1}{4}$in/0.75cm seam allowance. Using a rotary cutter and quilter's ruler, cut the bands into segments the same width as the original strips (diagram 1a).

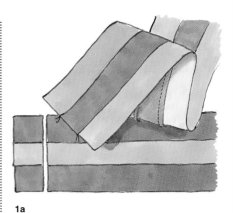

1a

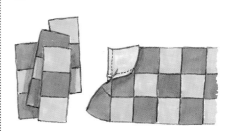

1b

3   Taking the usual seam allowance, stitch alternate segments together to form a new band (diagram 1b).

On-point Squares

You will need three fabrics: one light, one medium and one dark toned.

1   Cut a strip from the dark fabric including seam allowances, say $3\frac{1}{2}$in/9cm wide. Cut the other two fabrics to the same width plus $\frac{1}{2}$in/1.5cm.

2   Stitch into a band, with the dark fabric in the middle (diagram 2a). Using a rotary cutter and quilter's ruler, cut the bands into segments the same width as the middle (i.e. dark) fabric.

3   Join the segments together in a staggered pattern by dropping down one color each time (diagram 2b). Pin at the junctions of the squares, pushing the seam in opposite directions. Stitch right to the ends of each square. Press, trying not to stretch the fabric.

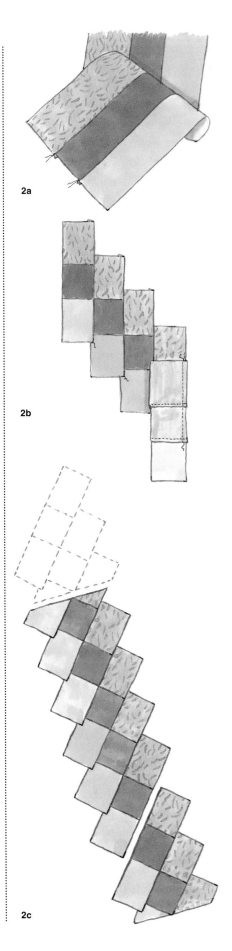

2a

2b

2c

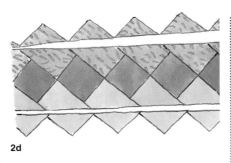

2d

4   To give the band straight ends, cut through the band vertically at the lefthand end, then move this section to the opposite end and join (diagram 2c).

5   Trim off the points at the top and bottom of the band, leaving a ¼in/0.75cm seam allowance on either side (diagram 2d).

Chevron Pattern

You will need two fabrics of contrasting colors: A and B. Fabric A will be cut to a narrower width than fabric B.

1   Cut strip A, 1½in/4cm wide and cut two strips of fabric B, 2½in/6.5cm wide.

2   Stitch into a band, with fabric A in the middle.

3   Carefully fold the band in half crosswise, pinning to match the seams. Using a quilter's ruler at 45 degrees across the band, make a cut across the band at the righthand end. Cut further segments across the band parallel to this and the width of the broader strips along the length. There will be some wastage (diagram 3a). You will now have segments at two angles.

4   Lay the segments on a work surface, alternating the angles, and stitch together, making sure the seams lie in opposite directions. Trim off the points (diagram 3b).

Band of Crosses

You will need two fabrics of contrasting colors: A and B.

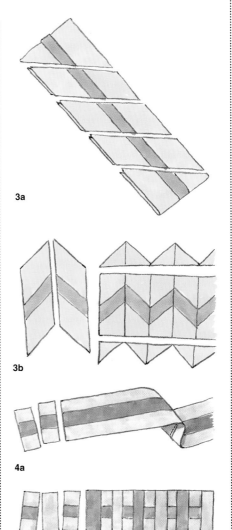

3a

3b

4a

4b

1   Cut two strips from fabric A and three strips from fabric B, each 1½in/4cm wide.

2   Using two strips of B and one of A, stitch into a band, with fabric A in the middle. Using a rotary cutter and quilter's ruler, cut the band into segments the same width as the original strips (diagram 4a).

3   Cut the remaining strips of A and B into 3½in/9cm lengths. Note that this is the same length as the depth of the segments cut in step 2.

4   Stitch into a new band, with alternate lengths cut in step 3 between the pieced segments (diagram 4b).

Tamiami Trail

THIS QUILT USES LARGE-SCALE TRADITIONAL SEMINOLE PATTERNS INTERSPERSED WITH PLAIN BANDS OF COLOR. I HAVE MADE IT UP IN A "HOT" COLOR SCHEME IN KEEPING WITH THE SEMINOLES' LOVE OF STRONG, BRIGHT HUES. THE CENTER OF THE QUILT IS MADE UP OF THREE MAIN AREAS DOMINATED BY THE DIAGONAL BAND. I HAVE QUILTED BY HAND, MAINLY "IN-THE-DITCH", SINCE THE PATCHWORK DESIGN ALREADY PROVIDES PLENTY OF SURFACE INTEREST. THE SIZE IS SUITABLE FOR A LAP QUILT OR TO COVER THE TOP OF A SINGLE BED.

Quilt size: 56 x 56in / 142 x 142cm

Materials

All fabrics used in the quilt top are 45in/115cm wide. Make sure you have a range of light, medium and dark tones.

- ▣ Brown paper
- ▣ Borders and pattern bands: 1½ yards/1.5m dark fabric A
- ▣ Main colors: 20in/50cm each of three fabrics: B, C and D

- ▣ Secondary fabrics: 1¼ yards/1.25m each of three fabrics: E (light tone), F (medium tone) and G (darker tone)
- ▣ Backing: 60 x 60in/153 x 153cm
- ▣ Batting: low-loft, 60 x 60in/153 x 153cm
- ▣ Quilting thread to match fabric A

DESIGNING

1 Tape sheets of brown paper together to produce a 45in/115cm square. This is the pattern master for the colored central area of the quilt. Crease the diagonal line from the top left to the bottom right corner. Measure 12in/30cm away from this line on both sides and draw lines parallel to it (diagram 1). Cut along these drawn lines to make three pieces.

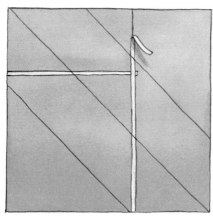

1

CUTTING AND STITCHING

1 Cut and reserve four border strips from fabric A, 6in/15cm wide and 56in/142cm long.

Tip *It is easier to cut these and all subsequent strips of A from the length of the fabric. Strips from all the other fabrics are cut from selvage to selvage.*

2 For the central diagonal check, cut three strips from fabrics A and B, each 2½in/6.5cm wide and 45in/115cm long. Use to make a checkerboard pattern strip (see page 136) at least 66in/130cm long.

3 For the on-point squares, cut a strip of fabric A, 3½in/9cm wide and 45in/115cm long. Cut one strip from fabrics E and F, each 4in/10cm wide and 45in/115cm long. Use to construct a band of on-point squares (see page 136).

4 For the chevron band, you will need strips 66in/168cm long, so if your fabric is 45in/115cm wide, join two lengths before cutting any strips. Cut a strip of fabric A, 1½in/4cm wide. Cut two strips from fabric B, 2½in/6.5cm wide. Use to construct a chevron band (see page 137), 4½in/11.5cm wide and 31in/79cm long.

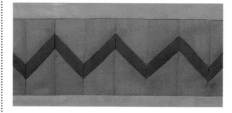

5 For the band of crosses, cut two strips from fabric D, 1½in/4cm wide and 28in/71cm long and three strips from fabric C, 1½in/4cm wide and 28in/71cm long. Use to construct a band of crosses (see page 137).

6 From fabric G, cut four strips, 1½in/4cm wide. Stitch one strip to either side of the checkered band and the chevron band.

7 From fabric D, cut two strips, 1½in/4cm wide. Stitch one strip to either side of the on-point squares.

8 From fabric A, cut two strips, 1½in/4cm wide. Stitch to either side of the band of crosses.

ASSEMBLING THE BANDS

1 Following the quilt assembly plan, make up the center diagonal section. Here you have free choice of the colors you use. All the narrow strips are 1in/2.5cm, finished width. The other widths are as indicated in diagrams 2 and 3 but remember to add ¼in/0.75cm seam allowance on each side when cutting strips. Make sure you stitch adjacent seams in opposite directions to avoid curvature.

2 Once the strips for the diagonal section have been stitched together, pin the center piece of the paper pattern over them and cut around, leaving an extra ¼in/0.75cm seam allowance on each side (diagram 2).

3 Following the quilt assembly plan, stitch the remaining bands into one large square, approximately 31in/80cm long. Note that if you make the two outer bands 6in/15cm wide, you will have plenty of fabric to play with. Place the two paper triangular sections on top and cut out, remembering to add the usual seam allowances all around (diagram 3).

FINISHING

1 Following the quilt assembly plan, stitch the three main sections of the top together.

2 Add the borders to first the sides, then the top and bottom of the quilt in the usual way (see page 21).

3 Lay out the backing, smoothing out any wrinkles, and lay the batting on top, aligning raw edges.

4 Lay the pieced top, right side up, then sew lines of basting about 4in/11cm apart across the quilt from

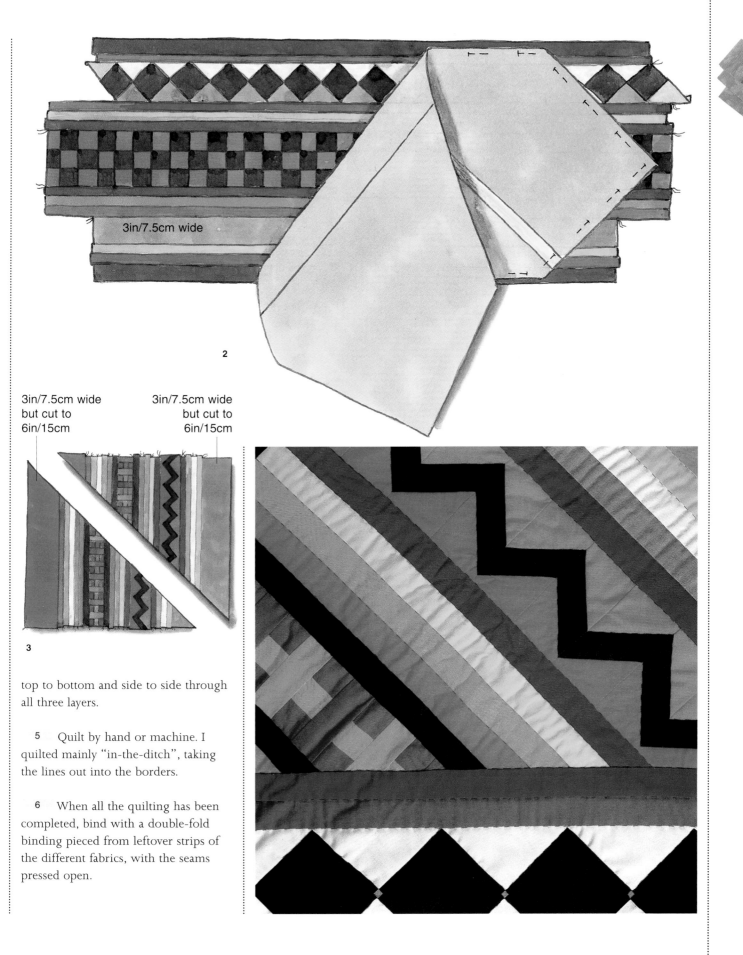

2

3in/7.5cm wide

3in/7.5cm wide
but cut to
6in/15cm

3in/7.5cm wide
but cut to
6in/15cm

3

top to bottom and side to side through
all three layers.

5   Quilt by hand or machine. I
quilted mainly "in-the-ditch", taking
the lines out into the borders.

6   When all the quilting has been
completed, bind with a double-fold
binding pieced from leftover strips of
the different fabrics, with the seams
pressed open.

BARGELLO QUILTS

The beautiful flame patterns in Bargello or Florentine tapestry have inspired quiltmakers to reinterpret the designs in fabrics and, with the advent of rotary cutting, Bargello quilts have become very popular.

They are made from strips cut across the width of the fabric, stitched together in color sequence, then sewn into tubes. The tubes are sub-cut into segments, which are opened out at different points to form new strips. These, when sewn together in a prescribed order, form the characteristic wave patterns.

The width of the strips depends on how many fabrics in the color sequence. For a balanced pattern, the color sequence needs to be repeated at least three times, therefore the more fabrics used, the narrower the strips.

FABRICS

As with most patchwork (see page 66), 100% cotton fabrics work best since they do not stretch or twist during sewing, they are easy to cut and mark, and the dyes tend to be more saturated, so that rich, dark colors are available.

Color Choice

Choosing the right colors is probably the most important element of the quilt. I find it easier to work with print fabrics rather than plain; prints tend to flow into one another, while plains stand out and become a focal point you may not have planned.

1   My favourite method is to choose the darkest fabric first, perhaps a rich green print, which includes secondary touches of other colors. This will be my accent color.

2   Next I choose a lighter green, then add in fabrics matching the secondary colors of the darkest fabric.

3   Finally, I choose one "surprise" fabric as a good contrast to all the others. This will give the effect of another pattern emerging and add "sparkle" to your quilt.

4   Lay the fabrics on a work surface, overlapping one another with the darkest to the left. Stand back to see if the colors flow into each other. Too little contrast between colors will make a very dull, uninteresting Bargello, whereas too much contrast will result in too much movement and the effect will be lost. You should choose between five and eight different fabrics for your first Bargello project.

5   When you have chosen your fabrics and the order in which they will be arranged, number them. It is a good idea to make a color chart by snipping off a little from each fabric and sticking this to a piece of cardboard showing the number of each fabric. This will serve as a useful guide later on.

Fabric Quantity

To calculate the width of the strips, decide on the finished depth of your Bargello quilt. For example, a wallhanging 36in/90cm long would need 18 strips, 2in/5cm wide, finished width. Therefore a color sequence containing six fabrics, repeated three times will give you the desired length.

To calculate how many strips to cut, count the number of times your color sequence repeats. If it repeats three times, you will need three strips from each fabric. One tube 44in/112cm wide, i.e. the whole width of a piece of fabric, will be sufficient for a quilt up to 28in/71cm wide, once seams have been stitched. If the quilt is wider than 28in/71cm, you will need to make more tubes to equal the width of the finished quilt without borders.

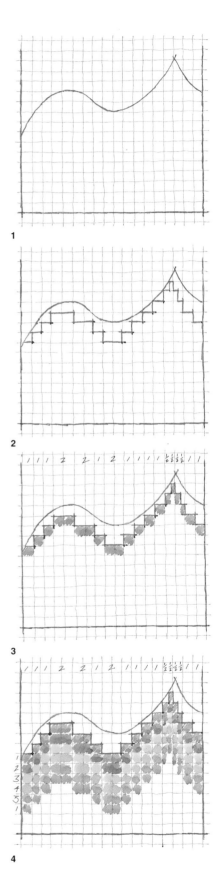

1

2

3

4

DESIGNING

1 Using graph or squared paper, mark the desired width of your quilt (each square will represent ½in/1.5cm) and draw a simple curved line across the middle of the design area. This first line will represent your darkest color. Your line can include more than one curve and can be graceful or include more dramatic "peaks" and "valleys". Practise drawing until you are satisfied with the result (diagram 1).

2 Following this curved line, draw another line along the outline of the squares on the paper to closely match your line. The horizontal line will cover more squares for graceful curves, and fewer for dramatic peaks and valleys. The vertical line should always be the same depth (diagram 2).

3 Next, using a pencil to match the fabric color, form squares to the depth of your chosen width of fabric. Note the width of each horizontal line at the top (diagram 3).

4 Now fill in the squares beneath this line, matching the color to your fabrics. Note the number of each fabric in the lefthand margin of your plan (diagram 4).

5 Count how many segments of each width you will need, i.e. three segments 2in/5cm wide, etc. and make a note of these.

CUTTING

1 First cut strips across the width of each piece of fabric to the chosen depth, remembering to add a ½in/1.5cm seam allowance to the finished width before you cut.

2 Using a rotary cutter and quilter's ruler, cut the desired number of strips (to equal the number of pattern repeats) from each fabric from selvage to selvage.

CONSTRUCTION

1 Lay the strips out in color sequence starting with no.1. Most fabrics vary a little in width, so keep one edge of all your strips as level as possible. Join no.1 to no.2 using an exact ¼in/0.75cm seam allowance. Do not pull or stretch the strips while sewing and sew with a stitch length of about 2.5.

2 Sew strip no.3 to strip no.2, starting at the opposite end. If you sew each strip in alternate directions it will help to stop your set of strips "bowing" in the middle.

3 Continue adding all the strips in sequence. When all the strips are joined, press the seams in alternate directions.

4 Next join the bottom fabric to the top fabric, right sides together, forming a tube, making sure that the tube does not become twisted and lays flat (diagram 5).

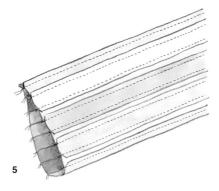

5

5 Now cut the tube into segments or rings. Lay the tube flat on a cutting mat (you can fold the tube lengthways if this does not fit onto your mat) making sure all seams are flat and straight, and using a rotary cutter, trim the lefthand selvage edges (see page 80).

6 Working from this straight edge, cut across the tube to produce segments to the widths previously

noted. It is easier to cut all segments of one width and then go onto the next width, i.e. cut all 2in/5cm segments, then all 1½in/4cm segments and so on. Pin all segments of one width together and label them.

7 Looking at your quilt plan and your color chart, select the segment of the width of the first column on the left of the assembly plan. Unpick the seam between the two colors that correspond to the top and bottom colors of this column (diagram 6). Lay this segment down to your left keeping the top fabric at the top.

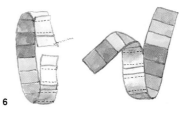

6

8 Continue unpicking between top and bottom fabrics for each segment and lay all segments down in their correct order according to your design. You can check for accuracy as each color should step up or down by one row to create the curves. When all segments are laid out, check that the colors run in the correct order.

9 Working from the left, begin joining the segments, again working in opposite directions to avoid "bowing". As the seams were pressed in alternate directions they should "lock" into position and should not need to be pinned. Press all the vertical seams to one side in the same direction.

10 If necessary, trim the top and bottom edges of the quilt to give a straight edge before adding borders.

11 Because of the large number of seams in a Bargello quilt, machine-quilt "in-the-ditch" following the lines of the design.

Bargello Wallhanging

THIS SMALL WALLHANGING IS AN EASY INTRODUCTION TO THE TECHNIQUE AND CAN BE PIECED IN A FEW HOURS. I HAVE CHOSEN A FLAME COLORED COTTON AS THE SURPRISE COLOR, SET OFF AGAINST A DARK PATTERNED FABRIC (THE ACCENT COLOR) WITH A HINT OF THE SAME COLOR AND THREE SHADES OF TURQUOISE.

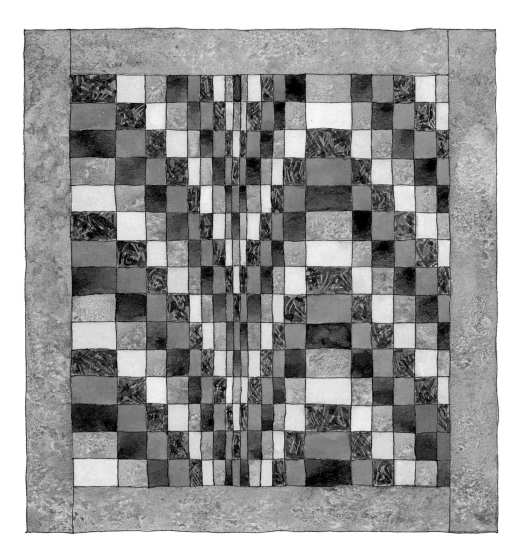

Quilt size: 30 x 34in/75 x 85cm

Materials

All fabrics used in the quilt top are 45in/115cm wide.

- ☑ Bargello fabrics: ¼yd/23cm of five different fabrics
- ☑ Border and binding fabric: ½yd/45cm
- ☑ Backing fabric: 1yd/85 x 95cm
- ☑ Batting: 2oz polyester, 34 x 38in/85 x 95cm
- ☑ Machine quilting thread

CUTTING

1   Number the fabrics 1 to 5, the darkest being number 1 and the lightest number 5. From each of the five fabrics, cut three strips from selvage to selvage, 2½in/7cm wide.

2   Trim off all selvages from both ends of all these strips.

STITCHING

1   Lay the strips of fabric on a working surface, with number 1 at the top and shading the colors down to number 5 at the bottom. Repeat this sequence twice more until all 15 strips are laid out (diagram 1).

2   Take strips 1 and 2 from the top of the sequence, place right sides together and stitch down one long edge, taking an accurate ¼in/0.75cm seam. Open out and press the seam upwards.

3   Take strip 3 and place on top of strip 2, right sides together and stitch as before. Open out and press the seam downwards.

4   Continue in this way being very careful to stitch accurate seams so that the strips are of even depth all the way across the width. Press alternate seams in opposite directions.

5   Place the stitched fabric on a cutting mat and, using a rotary cutter and ruler, trim the lefthand edge so that it is straight.

6   Using the lefthand edge as a guide, fold the fabric in half lengthwise with right sides together and stitch the final seam to form a tube. Press the seam (diagram 2).

7   Fold the tube flat and place on a cutting mat. Make sure that the lefthand edge is still at right angles to the seams (trim if not), then cut crosswise strips

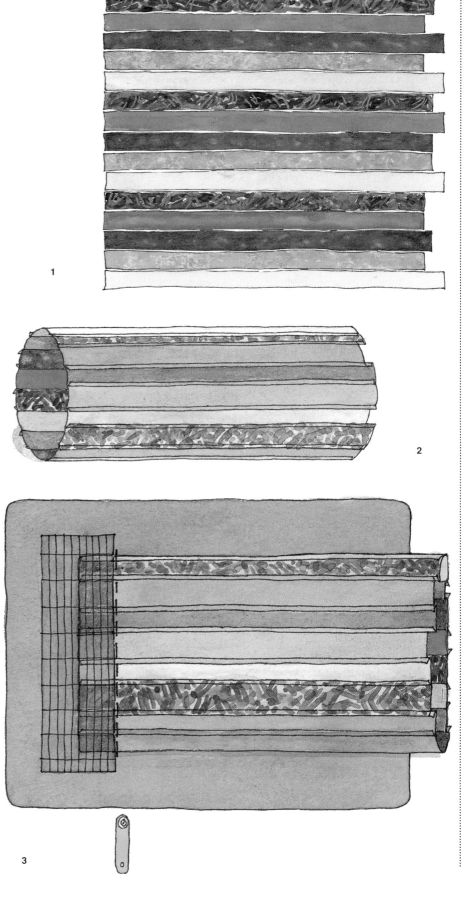

1

2

3

as follows (diagram 3):
4 x 3½in/9cm wide;
1 x 2½in/6.5cm wide;
7 x 2in/5cm wide;
7 x 1½in/4cm wide;
3 x 1in/2.5cm side.

8   Pin the strips of the same size together with a note of their width for ease of identification.

9   Referring to the chart opposite, unpick the seam between two fabrics and, working from left to right, lay these out flat, checking with the quilt layout that the colors are in the correct order.

10   Join the rows, starting from the left, carefully matching seams and being careful not to stretch the strips. Press gently with all seams to one side.

ADDING THE BORDERS

1   Determine the length of the two side borders by measuring the pieced top from top edge to bottom edge through the center. Cut two lengths from the border fabric to this measurement and 3½in/9cm wide.

2   Stitch the borders to the quilt sides. Press the seams towards the borders.

3   Determine the length of the top and bottom borders by measuring the pieced top from side edge to side edge through the center. Cut two lengths from the border fabric to this measurement and 3½in/9cm wide.

4   Stitch the borders to the top and bottom edges of the quilt and press the seams towards the borders.

strip	top fabric	bottom fabric
3½in/9cm	1	5
2½in/6.5cm	5	4
2in/5cm	4	3
2in/5cm	3	2
1½in/4cm	2	1
1½in/4cm	1	5
1½in/4cm	5	4
1in/2.5cm	4	3
1in/2.5cm	3	2
1in/2.5cm	4	3
1½in/4cm	5	4
1½in/4cm	1	5
1½in/4cm	2	1
2in/5cm	3	2
3½in/9cm	4	3
2in/5cm	3	2
2in/5cm	2	1
2in/5cm	1	5
2in/5cm	5	4
1½in/4cm	4	3

FINISHING

1   Lay the backing right side down and smooth out any wrinkles. Center the batting on top, then the pieced top, leaving a small margin of batting and backing showing around the edges.

2   Baste or pin the fabric sandwich together (see page 37). Because of all the seams which would be difficult to stitch through by hand, bargello is best quilted by machine. Quilt in-the-ditch (see page 40) following the lines of the waves of pattern.

3   Cut strips of binding 2in/5cm wide and use to bind the quilt with a single-fold binding.

CATHEDRAL WINDOW

Cathedral Window is a traditional form of patchwork, often done by hand (or at least, a good portion of it being done by hand), which creates an item that is complete without additional backing and batting. This aspect has much appeal for some quilters. It is also a great way to show off a fabric collection or small pieces of embroidery.

The addition of borders has often necessitated adding an extra backing to conceal seams. The system I use for adding a border doesn't require an extra backing, so if you decide to use exotic fabrics or luscious silks for the foundation squares, you don't have to cover them up.

GENERAL INSTRUCTIONS

1 The foundation square is always cut twice the finished size required, plus $\frac{1}{2}$in/1.5cm for seam allowances. Therefore, for a finished 3in/7.5cm square unit, cut the fabric 6$\frac{1}{2}$in/16.5cm square.

2 Cut the square to the required size. Fold the square in half, right sides together. Stitch the two short sides, taking a $\frac{1}{4}$in/0.75cm seam allowance (diagram 1).

3 Open up the unit along the unstitched edges. Align the stitched seams in the center and pin. Stitch along this edge, taking the usual seam allowance and leaving an opening in the center (diagram 2).

4 Trim all threads and trim excess fabric at the corners to reduce bulk. Press the seams open being careful not to press the folded edges (diagram 3). Turn the unit right side out.

5 Align the center seams and close the gap with a couple of stitches.

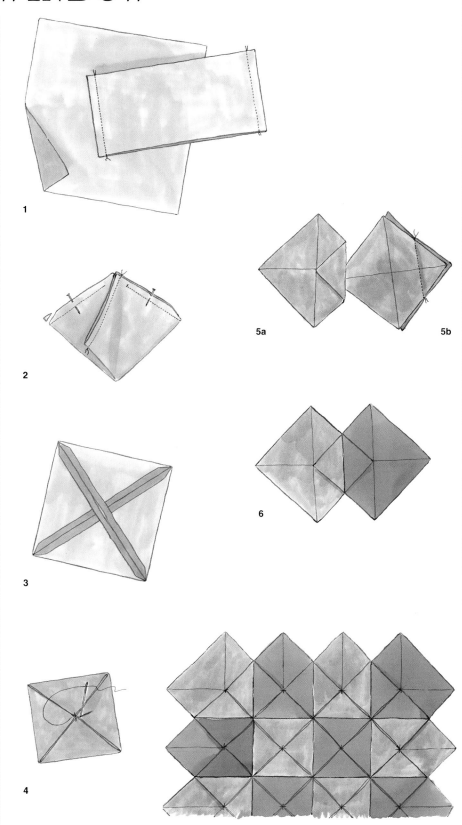

1

2

3

4

5a 5b

6

7

Traditional Method for Joining Units

6a Fold the corners into the center and stitch in place with a small cross (diagram 4). Make another unit in the same way, then place two units together, with either fronts (folded sides) or backs facing, and overstitch by hand to join them, using a matching thread and taking small stitches. Join units together in this way to form rows, then join the rows together.

Tip *If you are planning to add batting in the windows, stitch with the backs facing. This way the batting will hide your stitches.*

Alternative Method for Joining Units

6b Follow steps 1 to 5 above. Find the center point of each edge and mark with a pin. Fold one corner to the center and gently finger press the fold (diagram 5a). This will give you a line on which to stitch. Place two units together, wrong sides together and aligning pins. Stitch together by hand or machine, along the creased line (diagram 5b). Open up the seam and lightly press but only on the seam line itself (diagram 6). Continue adding units in this way, then add the rows together. Stitch the corners together in the center of each square in the traditional way.

Note *For either method: do not stitch the corners on the outside edges of the quilt top into the center of their units (diagram 7). Leave these free to allow for the addition of a border later.*

7 Cut a fabric "window" to the same size as the diagonal square formed between two folded foundation squares. Pin this square in position, trimming it slightly, if necessary, so that it doesn't extend over the adjacent sides (diagram 8).

Note *If using batting, place a square the same size as the "window" underneath the "window".*

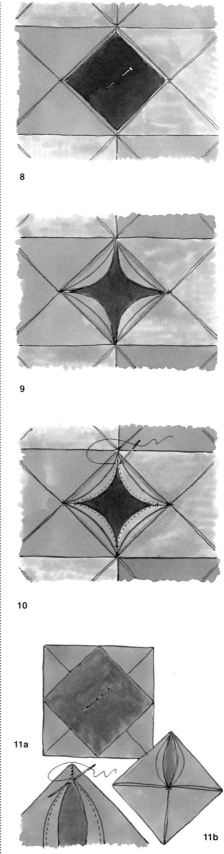

8

9

10

11a

11b

11c

8 Starting in a corner of this unit, roll the background fabric from underneath up over the edge of the window fabric (and batting). Don't be afraid to roll this edge back as far as possible. It can be as much as ¼in/0.75cm in the center of the fold (diagram 9).

9 Using a thread to match the background fabric, stitch this rolled edge in place using either an invisible appliqué stitch (see page 51) or a small evenly spaced backstitch. The stitching will go through the rolled edge of the background fabric, the window fabric and, if desired, into at least one layer of the background fabric on the foundation unit.

10 Make a bartack at the corners of the rolled edges to hide the raw edges of the window fabric (diagram 10).

SECRET GARDEN VARIATION

1 Make the foundation unit following steps 1 to 5 above. Cut the filler fabric for this variation to the same size as the finished foundation unit. Place the filler fabric on point in the center of the foundation unit (diagram 11a). (If using batting, place it under the filler square.)

2 Fold the corners of the foundation unit to the center and secure with a couple of stitches as in diagram 4.

3 Roll back the folded edges of the unit in the same manner as for Cathedral Window (diagram 11b), except that the folds must be stitched together at the corners for ¼in/0.75cm to conceal the raw edges of the Secret Garden filler fabric (diagram 11c).

ADDING BORDERS

1 Decide on the finished width of the borders and double this measurement, then add ½in/1.5cm seam allowances. This is the width to cut the border strips.

2 Measure the length of the pieced top, then measure the width. Add twice the finished width of the border and ½in/1.5cm seam allowance. This is the length. Cut border strips to match these measurements.

3 Mark the lengthwise center on the wrong side of one of the border strips. Fold the strip in half crosswise to find the center. Measuring from the center out, measure the finished border length required (the distance between the corners of the patchwork) and mark this measurement on the drawn line with a dot at each end. Using a

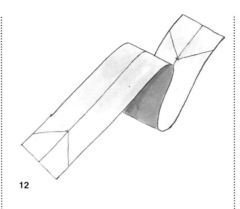

12

13

14

15

ruler with a 45° line, draw lines as shown (diagram 12). Repeat on the three other border strips.

4 Place the marked border strip, right side up, on a work surface. Place the patchwork on top, also right side

up. Place a pin through the corner of the patchwork to the dot marked on the border fabric. Repeat at the other end. Using pins, align the fold lines on the Cathedral Window units with the center marked line on the border (diagram 13).

5 Stitch the border to the patchwork along this line. Repeat on the other three sides.

6 Fold the work, so that two adjacent sides of the border align. Right sides of the border will be facing each other and the right side of the patchwork will be uppermost. Be sure to have all portions of the patchwork clear of the border strips. Align all the drawn lines and secure with pins. Carefully stitch along the lines drawn to create the mitered corners (diagram 14).

7 Open out and check to see that the corner is stitched correctly. Adjust if necessary. Now trim the excess border fabric, leaving a ¼in/0.75cm seam allowance at the corners forming the double miters. Clip the seam allowances into the "V" shape.

8 Press the seam open. Fold the border fabric up and away from the patchwork, aligning the two raw edges. There is now a complete border on the front and on the back.

9 If quilting the border, mark the design, then cut a strip of batting to the correct size, lay inside the border pieces and baste the three layers together.

10 Complete the window units around the edges by folding the remaining corners to the center of each unit. Stitch the corner points together and roll back the edges if appropriate (diagram 15).

11 Quilt your marked design. Remove basting and bind the edges.

Turquoise Windows and Bali Gardens

THESE TWO SMALL WALLHANGINGS USE BOTH THE STANDARD METHOD AND THE VARIATION DESCRIBED ON PAGES 149 AND 150. "TURQUOISE WINDOWS" JUST USES THE CATHEDRAL WINDOW TECHNIQUE, WHILE "BALI GARDENS" USES A MIXTURE OF THIS AND SECRET GARDEN.

Turquoise Window quilt size: 21¼ x 21¼in / 54 x 54cm

Bali Gardens quilt size: 21 x 21in / 53 x 53cm

Materials

All fabrics in both quilt tops are 45in / 115cm wide

Turquoise Windows:

☑ Background fabric: 2 yards / 2m

☑ Windows: sixteen pink squares; twenty yellow squares; twenty-four blue squares, all 2in / 5cm

☑ Sewing thread to match the background fabric

☑ Batting: low-loft, four 1½ x 22in / 4 x 56cm strips

☑ Quilting thread

Bali Gardens:

☑ Background fabrics: 1½ yards / 1.5m brown batik print; ¾ yard / 75cm blue batik print; four 6½in / 16.5cm squares of green batik print

☑ Filler fabrics: four yellow squares; twenty turquoise squares, all 3in / 7.5cm

☑ Window fabrics: sixteen pink squares, 2in / 5cm

☑ Sewing thread to match the background fabrics

☑ Batting: low-loft, four 1½ x 22in / 4 x 56cm strips

☑ Quilting thread

TURQUOISE WINDOWS STITCHING

1 Cut thirty-six 6½in/16.5cm squares from the background fabric.

2 Stitch and turn each square. Bring the corners to the center and stitch. Remember to leave the corners on the outside edges unstitched to allow for the borders.

3 Stitch these units into a grid of six units across and six rows using your preferred method of joining the units.

4 Following the quilt assembly plan, fill in the window spaces. Roll back the edges and stitch.

ADDING THE BORDERS AND FINISHING

1 Check the measurement of the side of the patchwork from corner to corner. It should measure 18in/46cm. If so, cut four strips of background fabric 3½ x 22in/9 x 56cm, otherwise adjust the border length to fit. Attach the borders to the patchwork. Mark the quilting design as shown in diagram 1.

2 Complete the window units adjacent to the borders.

3 Add the batting strips between the borders and baste in place. Quilt the borders and background triangles, then add a double-fold binding.

BALI GARDENS STITCHING

1 Cut the following 6½in/16.5cm squares from the background fabrics: twelve brown, twenty blue and four green.

2 Stitch and turn the brown squares. Bring the corners to the center and stitch.

3 Stitch and turn the blue and green squares. Place the filler fabrics in

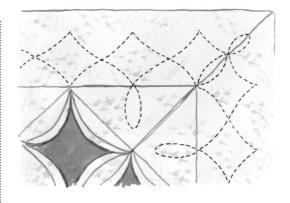

1

2

3

position, following the quilt assembly plan for color placement, then bring the corners to the center and stitch. Remember to leave the corners on the outside edges of the blue squares unstitched to allow for the borders.

4 Following diagram 2, stitch the units together using your preferred method in a six by six unit grid.

5 Fill the Cathedral Window units using the 2in/5cm squares, following the quilt assembly plan. Roll back all the appropriate edges and stitch.

ADDING THE BORDERS AND FINISHING

1 Check the measurement of the sides of the patchwork from corner to

corner. It should measure 18in/46cm square. If so, cut four strips of brown background fabric 3½ x 22in/ 9 x 56cm, otherwise adjust the border length to fit. Attach the borders to the patchwork. Mark the quilting design as shown in diagram 3.

2 Complete the garden units adjacent to the borders.

3 Add the batting strips between the borders and baste in place. Quilt the borders, then add a double-fold binding.

Yo-Yo Quilt

THIS PIECE DEMONSTRATES THE YO-YO TECHNIQUE. IT USES MANY DIFFERENT COLORS OF FABRIC AND SO IS MOST SUITABLE FOR USING SMALL LEFTOVERS. THE MORE COLORS USED, THE MORE INTERESTING THE PIECE WILL BE. A NUMBER OF DIFFERENT FABRICS ARE SUITABLE FOR YO-YOS: STRIPED FABRICS ARE PARTICULARLY EFFECTIVE, AS ARE FINE SILKS, COTTONS AND TRANSPARENT FABRICS, SUCH AS VOILE, NET AND CHIFFON. THICK FABRICS, SUCH AS VELVETS AND CORDUROY, DO NOT WORK WELL FOR SMALL PUFFS, BECAUSE THEIR BULK PREVENTS THE PUFF FROM BEING DRAWN UP SUFFICIENTLY. USE FABRICS OF SIMILAR WEIGHT IN A QUILT. DRESSWEIGHT SILKS AND COTTONS ARE RECOMMENDED FOR THIS WALLHANGING. YO-YOS ARE ALSO KNOWN AS SUFFOLK PUFFS, YORKSHIRE DAISY, AND PUFF BALL.

Quilt size: 35 x 35in/90 x 90cm
Total number of puffs required: 576

Materials

- ▣ Fabrics for the puffs: individual puffs are constructed from 3½in/9cm circles of fabric, the following number are needed: yellow 4; orange 12; burnt orange 20; red 28; red/pink 36; pink/cerise 44; lilac/purple 52; pale/dark blue 40; turquoise/navy blue 136; apple green/dark green 56;

grass green/dark green 56; greys/blacks 92
- ▣ Sewing thread to match the fabrics
- ▣ Doweling approximately 35in/90cm long
- ▣ Two screw eyes

MAKING THE SUFFOLK PUFFS

1   Begin by making the puffs in the center of the piece. Cut four circles of yellow fabric with a 3½in/9cm diameter, this is roughly twice the finished size of the puff.

2   Using a strong thread that matches the color of the fabric, begin with a knot on the thread and a back stitch (this thread is going to be drawn up, and needs to be securely attached). Run a gathering thread around the edge of one of the yellow circles, turning a narrow hem (approximately ⅜in/0.5cm) as you sew. The stitches do not need to be tiny, two stitches to ⅜in/1cm is sufficient (diagram 1).

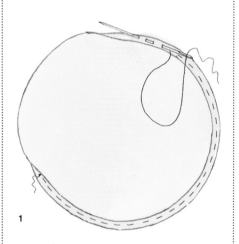

1

3   Draw the thread up tightly, secure with a knot, take the thread through the center of the puff and cut off. The end of the thread is then lost inside the puff. Flatten the puff, by gently pulling into shape (diagram 2).

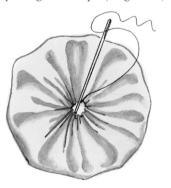

2

4   Following the quilt assembly plan and gradually working outwards in rows, make up the rest of the puffs in the colors specified and fix them in position on a pinboard.

5   As you work, keep standing back and viewing the piece to check whether any of the individual puffs do not blend in with the color scheme. If so, they can then be replaced or possibly used in a different position.

ASSEMBLING THE PUFFS

1   Once all the puffs have been made and you are pleased with the way the piece looks, begin sewing the puffs together in rows. To do this, place two puffs from one end of the top row, right sides together, then sew together with small oversewing stitches in a matching thread for a short distance along the edges (diagram 3).

2   Join all the puffs together in rows, then sew the rows together, in the same way.

HANGING THE QUILT

1   Cut the piece of doweling just slightly smaller than the overall size of the piece, then insert a small screw eye into either end.

2   Fix the doweling in place at the back of the quilt by making large stitches along the top row of puffs and over the doweling (diagram 4). The doweling can be hung from two picture hooks or nails inserted into the wall, using the screw eyes.

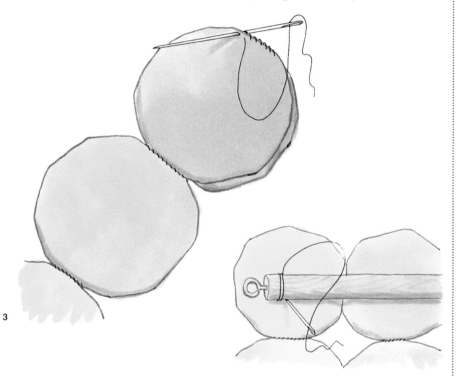

3

4

Note   Puffs can also be padded, by inserting a small amount of stuffing before the gathering thread is drawn up. After the thread has been secured, a small piece of the puff fabric needs to be pushed into the hole to prevent the stuffing from showing. This can be done using the points of some small, sharp scissors.

Puffs can also be joined in a circular arrangement.

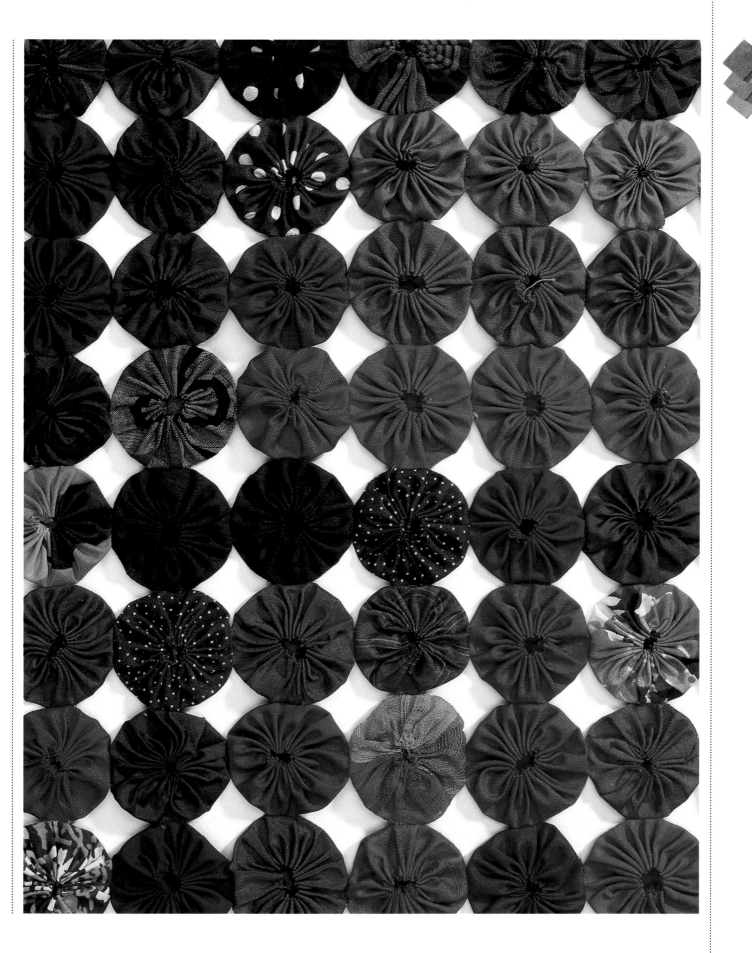

Folded Star Placemat

ALSO CALLED SOMERSET OR MITERED PATCHWORK, FOLDED STAR PATCHWORK INVOLVES FOLDING SQUARES
OR RECTANGLES OF FABRIC INTO TRIANGLES, THEN STITCHING THEM IN CONCENTRIC CIRCLES ONTO A
BACKGROUND FABRIC. IT IS BEST USED FOR SMALL PIECES, SUCH AS CUSHIONS OR PLACEMATS, RATHER THAN
WHOLE QUILTS, AS THE AMOUNT OF FABRIC USED MAKES IT HEAVY OVER LARGE AREAS. THE MOST SUITABLE
FABRICS ARE COTTONS, SILKS AND SOME POLYCOTTONS. AVOID FABRIC WHICH IS TOO THICK
OR DOESN'T TAKE A FOLD WELL.

Placemat size: 14½in/36.5cm diameter

Materials

- Background fabric: muslin, 16in/40cm square
- Folded fabrics: 49in/125cm red fabric; 1yard/1m red, green and gold patterned fabric, 45in/115cm wide
- Backing: red fabric, 16in/40cm square

- Compass
- Protractor
- Red sewing thread

CUTTING

1   Cut a strip of binding on the bias from the patterned fabric, 50in/127cm long and 2in/5cm wide.

2   Cut the squares for folding as described below.

1ST ROUND

1   Mark the muslin background square with diagonal lines from corner to corner to form a cross. Place the protractor on one of these lines, at the center point and mark an angle $11\frac{1}{4}°$ from the line. Draw a line through this point and the center across the square. Continue marking lines at $11\frac{1}{4}°$ until you have marked 32 lines (diagram 1).

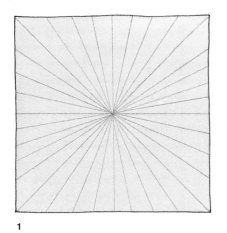

1

2   The rectangles of fabric for folding are always twice as wide as they are high, with $\frac{1}{2}$in/1.5cm seam allowance added to the height. Cut the first four rectangles of red fabric, $3\frac{1}{2}$ x $2\frac{1}{4}$in/9 x 6cm, on the straight of grain.

3   Take one rectangle and fold over the seam allowance along the top edge (diagram 2). Finger press or iron the fold in place.

4   Mark the center of the folded edge, then fold the two top corners downwards to the center bottom to make a triangle (diagrams 3a and b).

5   Press the folds firmly in position. It is important that the point

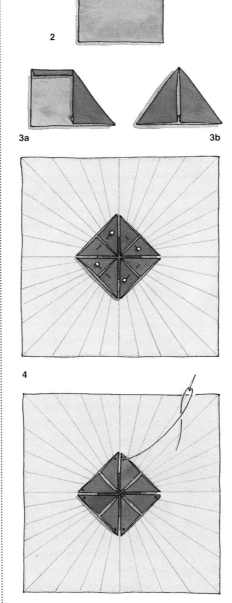

2

3a   3b

4

5

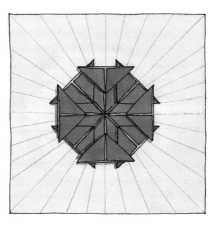

6

is a right angle. Repeat with the other three rectangles.

6   Place the four folded triangles on the muslin background square to line up with the vertical and horizontal lines, with the folded side facing up. The points should meet in the center. Pin in position (diagram 4).

Tip   *If your first pieces are a different color from the marked background (as here), place a $3\frac{1}{2}$in/9cm square of the same color underneath these four pieces to prevent any background from showing through.*

7   Attach sewing thread to the backing fabric close to the center point and bring the needle through to the front, taking it into the very tip of one of the folded triangles. Make a small stitch across to the tip of the opposite triangle and through to the back, making a small bar tack. This stitch should be hidden in the fabric folds.

8   Make another small bar tack in the same way to secure the two remaining triangle points, then stitch twice more over both bar tacks and take the needle to the back.

9   Bring the needle up again at the center base of one of the triangles, make two small stitches to secure, then repeat at each corner of the base.

Tip   *It helps to keep the stitches small and about $\frac{1}{4}$in/0.75cm away from the base edge. Do not pull too tight, as this might distort the work.*

10   Secure the bases of the other three folded triangles in the same way (diagram 5).

2ND + 3RD ROUNDS

1   Fold eight more triangles of red fabric. Place four triangles exactly over the first four but $\frac{1}{2}$in/1.5cm away from the center point. Place the next four in between, lining up the edges with the

diagonal lines of the muslin background square and the same distance away from the center point (diagram 6). Secure with three small stitches at the apex and stitches at three points along the base as before.

2   Place another round of eight triangles exactly over the last again with the points ½in/1.5cm below the previous points.

SUBSEQUENT ROUNDS

1   Place eight triangles exactly over the last, spaced as before. Place eight more triangles in between and the same distance away from the center point.

2   Continue in this way. On the seventh round only, increase the space between points to ¾in/2.25cm. On this round also, you will find that the spacing of the 16 triangles no longer covers the previous round at the base and this is the time to double the number of pieces from 16 to 32.

3   For the eighth round, you will need 24 red folded triangles and eight patterned fabric triangles. Place the red triangles first, then lay the patterned triangles on the 90° and 45° lines.

4   For the ninth row, you will need eight red and 24 patterned fabric triangles. Place these as shown on the assembly plan, laying the red first.

5   For the tenth row, you will need eight red triangles and 32 patterned. Place as shown on the assembly plan.

6   For the final row, you will need 32 patterned triangles. Place these as on the assembly plan.

FINISHING

1   Press the work from the back to smooth out the backing fabric. Using the compass, draw a 14½in/36.5cm circle on the back of the work.

2   Run a line of basting stitches just inside the marked line to hold down the last row of triangles, while you add the binding. Trim the placemat to the marked circle.

3   Cut a circle of red backing fabric to the same size. Using the patterned bias strip, bind the edges of the mat with a double-fold binding.

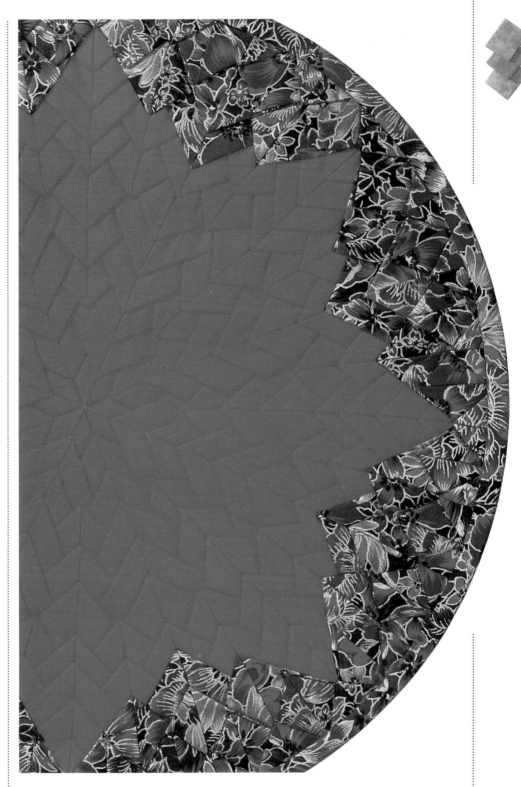

QUILT GALLERY

The following pages show a selection of the work of international quilt artists. They demonstrate how the techniques of patchwork, quilting and appliqué can be interpreted and embellished to produce highly individual pieces of textile art.

◀ Dinah Prentice
"Persephone Rising" 1992
120 x 168in/ 305 x 427cm

In the Greek myth, Persephone returns from the Underworld each Spring, triumphing over the powers of darkness. Persephone is represented by the central fork-like structure, juxtaposed with images depicting the exploitation and pillage of the natural environment. Calligraphic texts round the borders elucidate the quilt's message. Dinah Prentice uses the quilt medium to express radical feminist and political ideas.

Hand-dyed shantung silk. Hand-pieced, hand-quilted.

◀ Michael James "Fissure"
1998 44 x 69in/
112 x 175cm'

From the new body of work which Michael James began to develop in 1996. Inspiration is from many sources but particularly Mediaeval Russian icons and Amish quilts. The subtle variations in color and tone of hand-painted fabrics hint at natural processes of change and decay.

Hand-painted and tie-dyed African cotton. Machine-pieced and machine-quilted.

▶ Nancy Erickson "Hall of Memory #8 – The Ecstasy Which Occurs Upon Discovering the Cave Bear Ancestors" 1998 58½ X 60in/149 153cm

One in a series of quilts in which Nancy Erickson celebrates the wild creatures, specifically bears, with whom we share this planet but whose ways of life, and very existence, are threatened by the activities and ways of life of humans. The quilts are at once a celebration and a valediction. She sees herself as working within the rich tradition of the quilt as an expressive medium, one in which quilts have stories to tell, messages to convey.

Painted velvets, satins and cottons are appliquéd on shaped backgrounds, the works are layered and stitched by machine as quilts, then added to and backed as quilts, producing what she calls "quilteds", or painted quilts.

◀ Jo Budd "Oil Rig Module" 1996-8 102 x 126in/ 260 x 320cm

Jo Budd's quilt surfaces are visually related to abstract paintings but traditional patchwork quilts, especially those of the Amish, are a pervasive influence. The shapes, colors and textures observed on a prosaic object, a rusting oil rig, have been transformed into this artfully balanced surface. Translucent fabrics are hand-painted in a spectrum of colors, then layered to create subtle effects of color and shape.

Collaged and pieced hand-painted silks. Hand-quilted.

▶ Terrie Hancock Mangat
"Nutcrackers at Three
Madison Lane" 1998
62 x 72in/158 x 183cm

Terrie Mangat incorporates
many mixed media
techniques into her
quiltmaking, including
painting, embroidery,
appliqué, beadwork and
photocopying. The complex
and vibrant surfaces of her
quilts brilliantly reflect and
enhance their content,
which is densely packed
with references to personal,
religious and social themes.

This quilt is at once a
joyous celebration of the
artist's family unit
symbolized by the house,
and an expression of grief at
its loss after a broken
marriage. It is, she says,
"...part of my letting go of
my sadness..."

Oil paint on linen canvas,
hand-quilted with
embroidery thread. Gold
acrylic paint applied after
assembly.

◀ Elizabeth Busch "Fall
Study" 1997 32½ x
33in/82.5 x 84cm

This quilt is one of a series
of pieces interpreting the
seasons through color, shape
and movement. The series
marks a new direction for
Elizabeth Busch, inspired by
a conscious attempt to
simplify her work, focusing
on those elements and
techniques of quiltmaking
which she most enjoys: using
a grid, hand-painting, air-
brushing and hand-quilting.

Machine-pieced and hand-
quilted.

▲ Lynn Setterington "Means of Communication" 1998 83½ x 73½in/ 212cm x 186cm

Lynn Setterington draws inspiration from many quilting traditions, including the wholecloth quilts of the North Country of England, the richly textured quilts of Wales and the embroidered quilts, or kanthas, of Bangladesh. The content is inspired by the objects that surround us in our everyday lives, such as kitchen utensils, domestic equipment and cars, as well as by incidents and events in her own life. Contemporary imagery, like advertising or shop signs, may also be incorporated. The pieces are embroidered and quilted by hand because she has found that there is no other way to create the textural qualities she seeks.

Cotton fabric is appliquéd and hand-quilted.

◄ Diana Brockway "Heledd and her Sisters" 1997 41 x 66in/104 x 167cm

From an engraving by Harry Brockway to illustrate a Welsh folk tale. The quilt is an exploration of the effects of translating the original medium (engraving) into fabric while retaining the drama and expressiveness of the original. Modelling on faces was achieved by stencilling on white cotton, overlaid with silk habutai and black net, embellished with free-motion machine embroidery.

Machine-appliquéd and machine-quilted.

▲ Jane A. Sassaman "Flower Field" 1997 54 x 42in/137 x 103cm

Jane Sassaman's quilts are symbolic representations of the natural cycles and spiritual forces of life. Of this quilt, she says: "By using cartoon-like simplification of flowers and leaves I am attempting to express the creative energy, excitement and sheer joy of life."

Machine appliqué, commercial and hand-dyed cotton fabric, sheers and metallic synthetics. Machine-quilted.

▶ Sally A. Sellers "Chamber Music" 1998 39½ x 35½in/ 100 x 90cm

Sally Sellers has described her quilts as "intuitive collages sewn onto canvas." Her quilt art reflects and expresses her perpetual yearning for the security of order in a world which she recognises as inherently complex and disorderly. "All my work is an attempt to be at peace with this uncomfortable realization by imposing a temporary order and comfort." In "Chamber Music" these ideas are expressed in the interplay between the regularity of grids and stripes and the less-predictable liveliness of the uneven strokes.

Dyed, painted and commercial cottons are appliquéd on canvas. Machine stitching is used to add more color and texture.

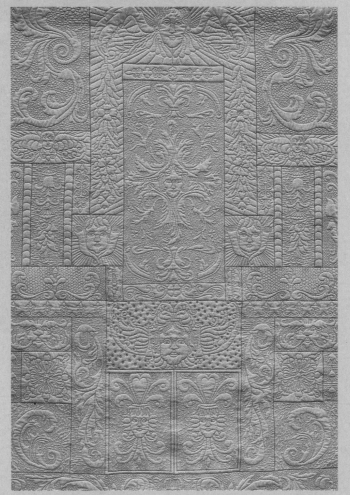

◀ Sheena Norquay "Baroque Babes" (detail) 1998 39 x 59in/99 x 150cm

A wholecloth quilt, the inspiration for which is taken from motifs on German Baroque furniture. It is finely quilted using the free-motion machine quilting for which Sheena Norquay is particularly noted. The use of gold thread on plain white muslin echoes the effect of elaborate gold decorations on plain, whitewashed church walls.

Muslin. Machine-pieced and free-motion machine quilting using gold thread.

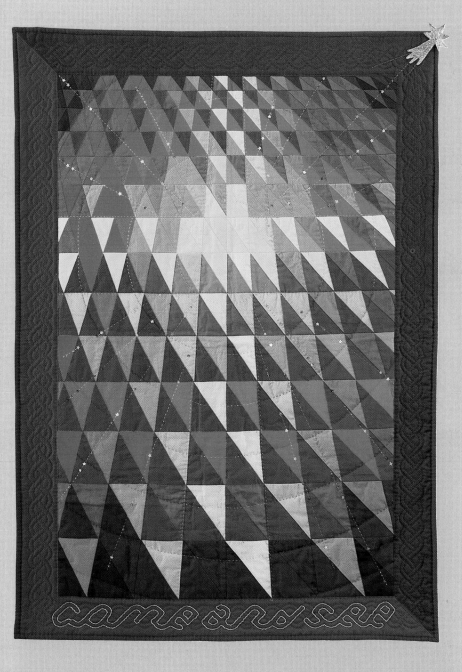

▲ Mary Catherine Lamb "Saint John as Eagle" 1998 33½ x 53in/85 x 134.5cm

The main inspiration is drawn from the Catholic ideology of the artist's childhood. The ideology has been rejected long since but the folkloric imagery of the church is embraced and manipulated with a mixture of affection and irreverence. The artist uses fabrics collected over many years, including curtains, tablecloths and garments with their homely, domestic associations - "vintage" fabrics. These are deliberately contrasted with exotic silks, satins, brocades and metallics which "lend an air of regal elegance ..." This is one of a series of four quilts interpreting the symbolic depictions of the Four Evangelists shown in the Book of Kells.

"Vintage" fabrics combined with commercial cottons, satins, silks and metallics. Machine piecing and machine appliqué. Embroidered and quilted with metallic thread.

▲ Louise Mabbs "Come and See..." 1996 24 x 36in/61 x 92cm

This title for this piece is taken from a modern hymn. All Louise Mabbs' work is informed and inspired by her religious convictions. Christian symbolism, such as crosses and stars, is interpreted in striking patchwork patterns, usually simple one-patch designs. The visual impact is achieved through imaginative use of color. A traditional Celtic interlaced design is hand-quilted round the border.

In this quilt the small patches, in the top six rows, are hand-pieced onto fusible webbing foundation blocks. Otherwise, machine-pieced and hand-quilted, with applied sequins on sun's rays. Cotton fabric throughout.

◀ Linda Straw "De Montfort" 1998
84 x 72in/214 x 183in

One of a series of five related pieces, entitled *A Thousand Years of British Quilt History*, commissioned by Madeira Threads UK. The whole work measures 35 x 6ft/10.6 x 18.3m. Inspiration for Linda Straw's work is drawn from literary and historical themes, in this case, the English Mediaeval period with particular reference to the De Montfort Parliament of 1265.

Her technique is basically reverse appliqué. Working from a cartoon, the design elements are transferred to fusible webbing which is incorporated into the work to stabilize the silk. The background fabric, appliqué shapes, batting and lining are assembled, then shapes are sewn from the back though all layers. The front is then embellished with machine embroidery.

▶ Siripan Kidd "Winter Blue" 1998
50 x 48in/127 x 122cm

Siripan Kidd's quilts are intensely abstract evocations of moods and emotions, inspired by, for example, her surroundings or the seasons. She begins with freely drawn shapes which, when she is satisfied with the proportions and balance of the design, are scaled up into a full-size cartoon on paper. This is then cut up and each piece is used as a template for cutting out the fabric, usually silk. The pieces are all joined by placing right sides together, then hand-stitching the seams.

Hand-stitched and hand-quilted in silk.

◀ Jan Myers-Newbury "Forest Floor"
1997 75ft x 62in/2.29m x 158cm

Jan Myers-Newbury's quilts express her
commitment to the pieced quilt form,
to constructing images from pieced
fabric. She works in a geometric,
straight-edged form, the lines being
softened and blurred by the artful
placing of tones and shades chosen
from a huge palette of subtly dyed
fabrics. Dyed fabrics are used because
she feels that in the dyeing process the
colors become an integral part of the
fabric. This use of pieced fabric satisfies
her intention to create textiles which
are unmistakably and essentially quilts,
in contrast to other techniques, such as
fabric painting or collage.

Tied, dyed and bleached cottons.
Machine pieced and machine-quilted.

▶ Pauline Burbidge "Paxton Study I"
1997 50in/127cm square

Pauline Burbidge's work explores and
celebrates aspects of the landscape and
environment in which she lives. This is
one of her "Reflections series", based
on photographic studies of the
reflections of light and water on the
River Tweed, near her home in the
Scottish Borders. (The title refers to the
name of a stately home in the area.)
   Innovative use is made of the
traditional patchwork block format,
each block being different yet subtly
related to the others. This enhances the
sense of moving light and water, which
is the immediate subject of the piece,
and at the same time inspires a
contemplative mood, as the eye is
drawn from block to block.

Cotton fabrics, including some hand-
painted and dyed, are backed with
fusible webbing. Shapes are freely cut
and applied, then the whole surface is
finely machine quilted.

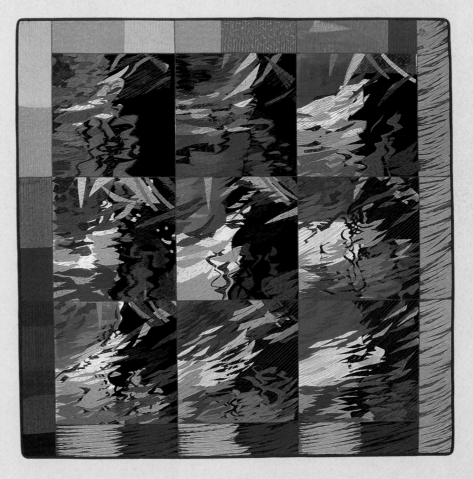

THE QUILTER AND THE COMPUTER

Information technology has revolutionized just about every aspect of our lives today: traditional crafts are no exception. Computer Aided Design (CAD) is a feature of most contemporary design courses, including patchwork and quilting.

Two distinct areas of computer technology have useful applications for contemporary patchwork and quilting. The first comprises a range of design and graphics programs which can be purchased as software, usually in the form of CD-ROMS. The second requires you to be connected to the Internet, which is a little more complicated.

Anyone with a suitable computer (PC) can buy and operate a CD-ROM. It is simply a disk which carries information and instructions. It can be loaded into the hard drive of your computer, provided you've got enough space there, or you can just use the CD-ROM like an ordinary CD, in which case you simply insert it into the appropriate drive to use it.

There are a great number of programs for planning and designing, many of which are intended for general use, drawing and coloring pictures, for example, and these can be used effectively for quilt design. There are also programs made specifically for patchwork quilters. Although the basic principles are common to all those available, there are variations in their specifications and functions, so it's worth doing a little research before buying. The best place to do this is at one of the bigger quilt shows where suppliers will demonstrate the available software.

In most of the programs, patchwork blocks can either be chosen from a library provided or you can draw your own. Blocks can be modified in any number of ways (see page 63). You can choose the colors you want to try out from a palette of colors and, with most programs, a palette of fabrics is also included. Some programs even allow you to scan your own fabrics into the computer, making it possible to try out various effects with the actual fabric you plan to use. All the measurements, including seam allowances, are automatically calculated at every stage. You can print out templates to whatever size you want, with or without seam allowances. You can print out the pattern, or any part of it, at any stage in the planning process

Most programs also include a selection of appliqué patterns and blocks which can be manipulated in the same way as the patchwork blocks.

The great thing about designing on the computer is the speed with which you can assess the effects created and, if you don't like what you see, change your mind.

QUILTERS ON THE INTERNET

Many quilters have been quick to take advantage of the Internet as a valuable resource for the exchange of ideas and information. For those who have yet to take the plunge, the Internet is simply a way of connecting your computer to a global network of computers. To be connected, you have to have a piece of computer equipment, called a modem, either attached to the computer or built into it, and a telephone connection. The connection has to be made through an Internet Service Provider (ISP) who will make a small monthly or annual charge. The day-to-day costs of being connected to the Internet depend on how much time you spend on it, reflected in your telephone bill. Fortunately, the amount of time is measured at the same cost as local calls.

This global network has thousands of pages of information and illustrations contained in websites - pages of information created by anyone who has the necessary software and technical know-how. Once you're connected, you can access any of these websites just by keying in its address, known as a Universal Resource Location, or URL. If you don't know the URL, you can find sites you're interested in by using the search engines, which are like electronic reference books or directories and which work at lightning speed.

There are hundreds of quilting websites, some just small, personal pages, some on the scale of the larger quilting magazines, with articles, information, patterns, ideas and advertisements. On most sites there are links to other related sites.

News Groups, or Chat Groups are a separate, but related, area of the Internet. These are a way of exchanging messages with other people with the same interests and there are thousands of them covering every imaginable area of interest. To join these, you simply choose the ones you're interested in, press a button and you'll receive all the messages posted by the other members of the Group. You can then send messages of your own which will be posted automatically to all the other members. Quilters have several such News Groups to choose from and they are an invaluable source of ideas and information as well as a way of making friends world-wide.

For some more specialized lists you need to subscribe, which simply means registering as a member but doesn't involve a fee. Specialist quilting lists include those for Quilt Art and for History and Heritage. These are particularly useful for research.

EXHIBITING QUILTS

There are two main types of exhibition. First, there are the quilt shows which accept and display all of the quilts which are submitted. At such shows you can see the whole spectrum of quiltmaking and quilters, from hobbyist beginner to consummate professional. These shows include a competitive element but if you don't want to compete you can usually stipulate on the entry form that your quilt is not to be judged.

Then, there are shows which are "juried". This means that only a selection of the quilts submitted are actually chosen for inclusion in the show. Shows of this sort often have a preliminary selection stage. You're asked to submit photographic slides of your quilts and a first judgement is made on the basis of those slides.

HOW TO EXHIBIT
How can you give yourself the best chance to win - or at least to make a good impression? The first and most useful thing you can do is to spend some time at quilt shows looking carefully at the winning quilts in the various categories. Ask yourself why each one is a winner in its particular category. What distinguishes it from the others in that group? Look at the design, the workmanship, the use of color. When it comes to planning and stitching your own quilts for exhibiting, these are some of the things you need to think about.

Entry Requirements
Read the entry requirements and the instructions about packaging, shipping and submission dates and make certain you comply with them. If hanging sleeves are stipulated, make certain that your quilt has one and that it's the right size.

Categories
At some shows there's a choice of categories in which you can enter your quilt. These include categories, such as those for "quilt art" or for "miniature quilts". Make sure you enter your quilt in the category which displays it to its best advantage. For example, bed-quilts, unsurprisingly enough, are often displayed and judged on beds. If your quilt is bed-sized but looks better on a wall, you might be wiser to enter it in another category – perhaps as a large wallhanging.

Details
When many quilts of very similar quality are on display it's often the details which decide the winner, so it's worth paying particular attention to the following:

• A quilt which is to be exhibited on a wall should hang straight, with even sides and neat edges. Irregularities become glaringly obvious when the quilt is seen at a distance.

• Judges are often very critical of bindings so pay particular attention to making them as neat and even as you possibly can.

• Batting should extend evenly into the binding. The binding itself should be of even width all around the quilt.

The only categories in which these details are less important are those such as quilt art, which are judged by other criteria. There, more attention is paid to creative use of design and color.

Quilting
Where hand-quilting is a feature of your quilt, it must stand up to careful scrutiny by the judges.

• If the quilting is entirely functional, what's important is not the actual size of the stitches so much as their uniformity (both in size and in positioning). Make certain, too, that they go through all the layers of the quilt.

• Judges frequently criticise a quilt for insufficient quilting when it's clearly intended to be quilted all over its surface but in fact isn't.

• Quilting which is decorative rather than functional will be judged on its appropriateness as well as its quality.

• Machine-quilting is judged on the same basis. That is, it needs to be technically skilled but also appropriate for the quilt to which it's applied.

JURIED SHOWS
If you're asked to send slides to a "juried" show, make sure they're of professional quality, as only such good quality slides will enable the selectors to identify the individual qualities which make your quilt special.

FINALLY
After the judging, you can usually ask for a copy of the judges' comments on your work. Study their assessment, both of your strengths and your weaknesses. You don't have to agree with them (judges are human and can make mistakes) but at least they should give you food for thought. Use what they've said to arrive at an objective appreciation of your current standards and situation.

CARE AND CONSERVATION OF QUILTS

The two biggest enemies to textiles are light and dirt. Whether your quilts are old or new, you can extend their lives by keeping them out of bright light and by keeping them as clean as possible.

Like all antique textiles, old quilts need special care and attention. Some of the processes necessary for cleaning and restoring textiles involve specialist equipment . Sometimes they also involve chemicals. Textiles requiring this sort of treatment are best left to experts. There are some basic repair and cleaning processes, though, which you can carry out safely, satisfyingly and satisfactorily at home.

In deciding how to treat an old quilt, the first step is to examine the whole quilt, back and front, to form an idea of its general condition. Was it made by hand or by machine? Are there any papers left in the patches? Is there any damage to it, such as fraying, holes or stains? Try to identify the fabrics used in the making of the quilt, including the backing and the batting. The nature of the fabrics will determine the methods of cleaning to be used.

CLEANING

Any quilt benefits from the regular removal of surface dirt and dust. Even washable quilts benefit from this treatment between washes. For delicate or fragile quilts, though, which can't be washed, this may be the only option. Use the flat head of a hand-held cylinder vacuum cleaner with the suction reduced to its minimum. Place a protective layer of fine fabric, such as nylon net, between the quilt and the cleaning head, which should be held just above the quilt surface. Don't rub or drag the vacuum head over the quilt.

WASHING

Although many antique cotton quilts can safely be washed, it's really a job for the experts unless you can be certain that all the fabrics your quilt contains are washable. Quilts which contain fabrics such as velvet or silk should never have water put on them, even for stain removal, because they may shrink or the colors may run. Chintz fabric, too, should never be cleaned with water because it will remove the sheen from the fabric. To check for color fastness, press a piece of damp cotton wool onto the fabric and see if any color comes off.

If you decide to go ahead with washing your quilt yourself, wait for a dry and breezy day. Support the quilt in a piece of clean white sheeting and immerse it in a bath of cool water. A small amount of gentle hand washing powder can be added to the water. Leave the quilt to soak for about an hour, using the supporting fabric to agitate it a little. To rinse, let the water drain away and refill the bath with clean water. Repeat the rinsing process until the water is clear. Then leave the quilt to drain sufficiently to be lifted out. Lay it out flat on a piece of sheeting to dry.

If washing your own quilt, which has been made with pre-washed fabrics and contains a washable batting, a washing machine can be used. You need to be careful, though. Try to choose a dry and breezy day. Use the gentlest washing cycle available and a short spin. The program for woollens is usually a suitable program to use. Dry the quilt either by folding it over a washing line or by spreading a large cotton sheet over a flat area and laying the quilt out on it.

STORING

If quilts are to be stored, following some simple rules will make sure they stay in good condition.

• The best way of storing any quilt is flat, on a bed. If it's an old quilt, particularly if it's fragile, keep it covered with clean white sheeting.

• Quilts can be stored folded but in this case rolls of acid-free tissue paper should be inserted into the folds to prevent creases forming. Quilts stored like this should be unfolded regularly, examined for signs of damage (for example from moths or damp) and re-folded in a different direction.

DISPLAYING OLD QUILTS

Fragile textiles of any sort should be displayed only for short periods and during that time exposure to light should be kept to a minimum. They should be well-supported by a batten passed through a sleeve.

INDEX

ACKNOWLEDGMENTS

The Publishers would like to thank the following for their help with the production of the book:

Bogod Machine Company
50-52 Great Sutton Street
London EC1V 0DJ
(for the loan of sewing machine feet)

Quilt Basics
Unit 19 Chiltern House
Waterside
Chesham Bucks HP5 1PS
(for the loan of fabrics and equipment)

The Quilt Loft
9/10 Havercroft Buildings
North Street
Worthing West Sussex BN11 1DY
(for the loan of fabrics and equipment)

Sue Scott for the quilting samples

Edwina Mackinnon for stitching the Mini Trip Around the World quilt

The quilt artists featured in the Quilt Gallery (pages 162 – 169). Copyright in these photographs is as follows: Diana Brockway p. 165 tr; Jo Budd p. 163 b; Pauline Burbidge p. 169 b; Elizabeth Busch p. 164 b; Nancy Erickson p. 163 t; Michael James p. 162 b; Siripan Kidd p. 168 b; Mary Catherine Lamb p. 167 r; Louise Mabbs p. 167 l; Terry Hancock Mangat p. 164 t; Jan Myers-Newbury p. 169 t; Sheena Norquay p. 166 b; Dinah Prentice p.162 t; Jane A. Sassaman p. 165 b; Sally A. Sellers p. 166 t; Lynn Setterington p. 165 tl; Linda Straw p. 168 t.

SUPPLIER

Barbara Howell
Cae Cam, Ochr'y Bryn, Henllan
Denbighshire LL16 5AT, U.K.
(printed paper bags)